Gluten-Free
Cupcakes

GLUTEN-FREE

Cupcakes

50 Irresistible Recipes Made with Almond and Coconut Flour

Elana Amsterdam

Photographs by Annabelle Breakey

CELESTIAL ARTS
Berkeley

Some of the recipes in this book include raw eggs. When eggs are consumed raw, there is always the risk that bacteria, which is killed by proper cooking, may be present. For this reason, always buy certified salmonella-free eggs from a reliable grocer, storing them in the refrigerator until they are served. Because of the health risks associated with the consumption of bacteria that can be present in raw eggs, they should not be consumed by infants, small children, pregnant women, the elderly, or any persons who may be immunocompromised. The author and publisher expressly disclaim responsibility for any adverse effects that may result from the use or application of the recipes and information contained in this book.

Copyright © 2011 by Elana Amsterdam
Photographs copyright © 2011 by Annabelle Breakey

Published in the United States by Celestial Arts, an imprint of the Crown Publishing Group, a division of Random House, Inc., New York.
www.crownpublishing.com
www.tenspeed.com

Celestial Arts and the Celestial Arts colophon are registered trademarks of Random House, Inc.

Library of Congress Cataloging-in-Publication Data

Amsterdam, Elana.
  Gluten-free cupcakes : 50 irresistible recipes made with almond and coconut flour / Elana Amsterdam.
     p. cm.
  Includes index.
  Summary: "A collection of 50 gluten-free cupcake recipes featuring coconut flour and almond flour"
—Provided by publisher.
1. Gluten-free diet—Recipes. 2. Cupcakes. 3. Cooking (Almond flour)
4. Cooking (Coconut flour) 5. Cookbooks. I. Title.
  RM237.86.A474 2011
  641.5'638—dc22
                          2010045093

ISBN 978-1-58761-166-7

Printed in China

Design by Betsy Stromberg
Food styling by Dan Becker
Food styling on pages 25 and 54 by Karen Shinto
Prop styling by Emma Star Jensen
Food styling assistance by Emily Garland and Jeffrey Larsen

10 9 8 7 6 5 4 3 2 1

First Edition

Dedication

To my mother, who introduced me to the world of cupcakes and taught me confidence in the kitchen.

Contents

Acknowledgments

I am grateful to so many people for their help in putting together this book. First, thank you to my darling husband, for tasting every creation I concocted week in and week out. Second, thank you to my two sons, J and E, for their constant enthusiasm and creative input, and for bringing their friends around to sample the cupcakes.

I'd also like to thank my amazingly talented agent, Alison Schwartz; my fabulous editor, Sara Golski, with whom I have truly enjoyed collaborating on this book and the last; and the fantastic Annabelle Breakey, for her incredible photography. Thanks also to Ezra and Beulah Amsterdam, Dina Amsterdam, Marylyn Dintenfass, John Driscoll, Karin Lazarus, Jennifer French, SDK, Patrick Jelliffe, Leah Capezio, Leah Biber, Karen Shinto, Dan Becker, Emma Star Jensen, Jeffrey Larsen, Emily Garland, and Betsy Stromberg.

Finally, thanks to Helen for support, encouragement, and thirty years of friendship.

Introduction

*F*airy cakes, baby cakes, patty cakes, little cakes . . . whatever you call them, cupcakes are a diminutive, delightful dessert. I love cupcakes; they have a special place in my heart. In fact, like many in this country, I'm slightly obsessed with them.

The first object of my cupcake affection was Magnolia Bakery in New York City. Back in the early nineties, every time I was in the Village, I made sure to stop by this adorable bakeshop. On my excursions down to Magnolia (I lived on the Upper West Side of Manhattan for nearly twenty years), I concluded that there are two types of people—cake people and frosting people. While Magnolia had fabulous cakes, their frostings were even better—actually, they were obscenely good. And what better way for one person to eat a large amount of frosting than piled on top of a delicious cupcake?! I was madly in love with Magnolia.

This particular affair ended abruptly. In 1998 I discovered I had celiac disease (a multi-organ autoimmune disorder triggered by ingesting gluten). This diagnosis spurred me to bake gluten free for myself, from scratch. So I began to make my own cupcakes. Even though the cupcake is typically a gluten- and dairy-filled dessert, people with food intolerances hanker for this delightful little treat just like everybody else. Two children and many birthday parties later, my passion for cupcakes has not cooled one bit, and I am still smothering them in frosting.

While my family loves cupcakes just as much as the next, there are a number of us with food restrictions. My older son also has celiac disease, as do my sister, mother, and mother-in-law. My younger son is gluten-intolerant.

As you can imagine, gluten-free cooking is near and dear to my heart (as is celiac education and awareness). My husband, on the other hand, has no food restrictions whatsoever—though he definitely prefers a nutrient-dense, high-protein snack. I also have many friends who have an intolerance to dairy. So when I bake, I'm looking to create something that satisfies everyone's needs—gluten free, dairy free, low in sugar, and high in protein. That's a lot of criteria to meet! Luckily, I like a good challenge.

In May 2010 my romance with cupcakes became more public—and more involved. I featured cupcakes on my blog, elanaspantry.com, creating a "Month O' Cupcakes." That month-long cupcake project became the basis for this book, as I experimented to find even more cupcake and frosting flavors to satisfy the growing gluten-free audience. My children and I went through every cupcake book we could get our hands on in order to determine the "must have" types of cupcakes for "our" book, and then I set out to create gluten-free versions that rely on only a handful of natural ingredients.

My cupcake obsession did not skip a generation. Not even close. My children love cupcakes just as much as I do. My older son is a chocolate boy. It was he who decided that we needed Marble Cupcakes (page 27), and he went on to pre-test this creation and write up very professional notes along the way. My younger son loves anything that is edible and pink. He does a fine job when it comes to licking clean bowl after bowl of Strawberry Meringue Frosting (page 97).

My boys were also the inspiration for the Special Occasion section of this book. They love complicated, gooey confections and I love making such treats in a healthier form—hence this section was born. The Special Occasion cupcakes do have more steps than those in the rest of the book, however they are quite impressive visually and are beyond decadent.

While my children were focused on fancy, fun, showstopping cupcakes—such as the Banana Split (page 77)—I was determined to come up with a delicious vegan cupcake. Cooking without the gluten from wheat flour, the fat from butter, and the protein from eggs is not an easy task. I sometimes joked with my friends (and Facebook followers) that I was creating a recipe out of thin air. Forty-nine test batches later, I was finally satisfied with my gluten-free Vegan Chocolate Cupcakes (page 23). I was determined to make this vegan treat so that readers would be able to use it for the Special Occasion recipes in this book. With a variety of vegan frostings, a vegan cupcake was necessary to round out the offerings.

In addition, I slipped in several "savory cupcakes" to the recipe mix, which I'm calling "muffins." After baking so many sweet cupcakes, I couldn't resist adding a few savory, because it's not always easy to find great gluten-free muffins.

Naturally, all of the recipes in this book are *strictly* gluten free (gluten is a protein found in wheat, rye, and barley). You will not find a recipe here that calls for even an ounce of gluten.

As for other food restrictions, there are the vegan cupcakes that I mentioned above, plus an assortment of dairy-free and vegan frostings and fillings, so that all of you can break bread with as many friends as possible, regardless of dietary restrictions. That's always my goal.

Finally, a couple of tips on how to use this book. I have included a sweetness rating for each of the cupcake recipes here. This rating will let you know which cupcakes are less sweet and better for something such as brunch or a snack, and which recipes are very sweet and entirely decadent treats best saved for a festive dessert. Although I give suggestions for frostings at the top of most of the cupcake recipes, you can mix and match to your heart's desire. Feel free to get creative with pairings other than those I have suggested.

Happy baking!

Cupcakes 101: Equipment, Tips, and Ingredients

Much can go wrong when baking cupcakes. This I learned along the way in creating an entire book about them. So, I have to give major credit to the writers of *Vegan Cupcakes Take Over the World*. Almost everything I learned about troubleshooting the little cakes came from them. Many thanks to Isa Moskowitz and Terry Romero!

I often receive questions about baking cupcakes at various altitudes and am asked if adjustments are necessary. Thankfully, this is not the case. I've tested many of these recipes at both mile high and sea level. So, please note that if your cupcakes are not turning out, an altitude adjustment is not the solution. See some of the other recommendations I list to help you figure out what the issue may be.

EQUIPMENT

Creating great cupcakes requires the use of certain tools. Nothing too fancy is needed here; these are just a few notes to let you know what equipment I keep my kitchen stocked with to achieve perfect little cakes.

Blender

A few recipes in this book require a "high-powered" blender. I use the Vitamix brand, though Blendtec will work equally well.

Glass Jars

I store all of my flours (and all of my dry ingredients) in glass jars in order to keep them fresh and maintain optimal moisture content. I have found that almond flour and coconut flour can be stored in tightly sealed glass jars in the refrigerator or freezer for several months.

I keep a $^1/_2$-cup measuring cup in the almond flour and a $^1/_4$-cup measuring cup in the coconut flour. I have quite a few sets of measuring cups so that my two boys and I can be making different recipes at the same time and have all the cups that we need—without sharing!

Handheld Mixer

I use an electric handheld mixer in most of the cupcake and frosting recipes in this book, other than a few that call for hand mixing of ingredients.

Measuring Cups

I use metal measuring cups for both wet and dry ingredients—the old-fashioned kind like my mom used. While general baking guidelines suggest using a liquid measuring cup for liquids to avoid spilling and also because there's a handy spout for pouring, I prefer to use the dry measuring cups for all of my ingredients. First, having glass around when my children are baking is a bit of a risk. Sometimes the kitchen gets crowded and we get a little wild (imagine ingredients flying everywhere). Second, I find that using less equipment, and fewer different types of equipment, simplifies and streamlines the baking process, thus enhancing my creativity. Lastly, I use the metal measuring cups instead of plastic because plastic is made from petrochemicals that contain endocrine-disrupting compounds.

Measuring Spoons

I find that a rounder, deeper set of measuring spoons works best. With less surface area on top, there is a smaller chance for measuring inaccurately.

Again, I use metal measuring spoons rather than plastic. I find that metal equipment wears well and lasts longer than plastic.

Microplane Zester

Given that I try to stay away from fruit-flavored extracts and flavorings as much as possible, and prefer less processed ingredients such as zest in both my cupcake and frosting recipes, I highly recommend this tool to speed your prep work. Another trick? Use citrus zest as an alternative topping to sprinkles; it's naturally beautiful, deliciously flavorful, and rich in health-building bioflavonoids to boot.

Mixing Bowls

I use one large and one medium mixing bowl for these recipes. I also use a deep bowl (made by Vietri) for making whipped cream and meringues; unlike other bowls, this one is almost "V" shaped, rather than "U" shaped. Using a bowl that is deep and not very wide is a little trick of mine that helps in aerating cream and eggs in whipped creams and meringues. My boys refer to our Vietri as the "whipped cream bowl," and easily make a batch of whipped cream in it at the drop of a hat. They are fearless in the kitchen, and this bowl helps them!

Muffin Pans

I recommend using aluminum muffin pans for making your cupcakes—coated, silicone, and disposable pans will not yield the same results. I use both regular and mini-size muffin pans, depending upon the recipe.

Oven Thermometer

My recipe tester, Karin, went out and got herself three of these just to make sure her oven temperature was *exact*. I would suggest one, so that you know that your oven is baking at the correct temperature. I keep mine in the oven all the time to confirm that my oven is properly calibrated, and I am providing the correct temperatures. Baking is a science (unfortunately, for the less scientifically minded among us), and temperature is an important part of the equation. If your temperature is off, your results are likely to be off as well. This is one culprit that is often overlooked when the desired results are not achieved.

Spatula

I use a flexible rubber spatula to scrape every drop of batter out of a bowl of frosting or cupcake batter. I also use a spatula when measuring the cupcake batter into the lined muffin tins—it's a great tool for leveling out those $1/4$ cups of batter.

Timer

Be sure to time the cupcakes when you are baking them. There is a window of time in each of the recipes for cupcake doneness. When baking, everything can affect that window—from the weather outside to the climate in which you live. That's why I give a range for the baking times.

BAKING TIPS

Gluten-free baking can be quite different from "standard" baking, and different gluten-free flours can vary from one another greatly. Recipes using coconut flour have unusually high ratios of wet to dry ingredients—so high, in fact, that some people suspect a mistake in the writing of the recipe. Do not be deterred, though—cupcakes made with coconut flour are absolutely wonderful, and although batter made with this flour can be quite wet, the resulting cupcakes are delightfully fluffy. While ingredient ratios in recipes using almond flour look more "normal," the resultant batters seem a bit thicker than standard batters made with gluten.

A note on multiplying the recipes—when you want to increase the specified yield, I recommend that you make a second batch, rather than doubling the recipe.

When you are ready to bake, let the oven continue to preheat for at least 15 minutes once it reaches the necessary temperature. I know, this is a waste of energy; however, it will allow all the parts of the oven to come to the needed temperature, and your cupcakes will bake more evenly. Place your cupcakes on the middle oven rack, unless the recipe specifies otherwise. Lastly, please do not open the oven door every 2 minutes! This is a temptation for me every time I bake a batch of cupcakes, but opening the door to the oven changes the oven temperature and can ruin a good batch of cupcakes. Use the oven light if you have one and need to obsess the way I do, and don't peek until the lower end of the recommended baking range.

I do not recommend making cupcakes more than a day ahead of time. If you do want to make the cupcakes before needed, make them the evening before and allow them to cool in the pans overnight.

Coconut and almond flour cupcakes keep in slightly different ways. I leave my cupcakes made with almond flour out on the counter and they become more moist as the days pass. I live in the dry climate of Colorado—if you do this in a humid climate it may not work, so in that case I recommend you place your almond flour baked goods in an airtight container in the refrigerator after one day. On the other hand, coconut flour cupcakes cannot really be left out for more than 10 to 14 hours or they will harden and turn into rocks. Therefore, I like to store my coconut flour cupcakes in an airtight container in the refrigerator and recommend this for all climates. Frost just prior to serving. I don't recommend freezing any of the cupcakes or frostings—these desserts are much better served fresh.

MEASURING TIPS

I use the dip and sweep method for measuring flours, which entails dipping the measuring cup into the flour, scooping the flour into the cup, and then sweeping over the top with a spatula or knife to level off the measurement. Do not pour the flour into your measuring cup or it will yield significantly less flour than the recipe calls for.

If you prefer to weigh your dry ingredients, here is a list of weight measurements for various dry ingredients used in this book:

1 cup blanched almond flour = 4 ounces
$1/4$ cup coconut flour = 1 ounce
$1/4$ cup unsweetened cocoa powder = 0.7 ounce
1 tablespoon arrowroot powder = 0.3 ounce

I'm not suggesting that everyone needs to purchase a kitchen scale (though I have one and find it quite handy) and measure each ingredient in every recipe. I do suggest that if you are having trouble with the recipes, the accuracy of your measurements might be one angle to examine.

BATTER TIPS

Though these recipes are simple, a couple of points are in order when it comes to making the batters. First, use the recommended ingredients to achieve the desired results. Second, make sure your batters are thoroughly combined and do not overmix them. When the recipe calls for using a handheld mixer, do so. When a recipe calls for hand mixing, mix by hand. Using a stand mixer is not recommended because it can overmix ingredients and break down proteins, resulting in unseemly cupcake tops. Also, stop the mixer periodically and scrape down the bowl to make sure that all of the ingredients are incorporated.

If you find your cupcakes tend to sink in the middle, try adding an extra tablespoon of the specified flour—either coconut or almond, depending on the recipe. The flours used in this book are very, very new to the marketplace, and moisture content and quality can vary from brand to brand, and from shipment to shipment of the same brand.

Mixing batter made with coconut flour can be especially tricky. Make sure when you mix the wet ingredients into the dry ingredients and blend with a handheld mixer that there are no little lumps of flour at the bottom of your bowl. I like to remove the attachment from the handheld mixer and use it to whisk the bottom of the bowl to break up any remaining lumps.

On the other hand, be careful not to overmix. Stop beating when the batter is blended and the lumps have dissolved. Overmixing will break the protein in the eggs and cause the cupcakes to rise unevenly and look oddly stretched out on top. If this occurs, it means the cupcakes have risen twice—not a good thing. Overmixing your batter will result in cupcakes that not only look odd, but also taste rubbery.

FROSTING TIPS

Great cupcakes require great frostings, and also a variety of frosting options. While I have created some frostings that contain eggs and dairy, I have also created several vegan analogues. Further, there are several types of frostings in this book, including ganache, meringue, buttercream, and whipped cream. When using a thick frosting such as Chocolate Ganache (page 92) or Vegan Chocolate Frosting (page 92), apply a thick, smooth layer to your cupcake with a small metal frosting spatula or palette knife. For fluffy, airy frostings such as meringue or whipped cream, apply with swirls and texture using a butter knife or a large spoon to dollop. All of the frostings in this book are "pipe-able" and gorgeous when piped with a pastry bag. Frostings need to be a bit firmer when piped, so if you are planning to do this, chill your frosting a bit longer.

Always allow the cupcakes to cool for the recommended hour prior to frosting or removing from the liners. If cupcakes are frosted before they are completely cool, the frosting will melt and slide off the cupcake. If you try to remove a cupcake from its wrapper when it is still warm, the cupcake may break apart or stick to the wrapper. I let my cupcakes cool in the pan (unless otherwise specified) and do not use a wire rack for cooling.

If your frosting is too stiff and thick, warm it in a bowl or jar over a bowl of warm water to loosen it up, and then whip it again with a hand-held mixer or stir it to a spreadable consistency with a spoon. If your frosting is too loose or wet, place it in the refrigerator for a few minutes to thicken up. If you are making a recipe that calls for the cupcakes to be refrigerated immediately after frosting, then do so in order to keep the proper consistency of the frosting.

Meringue frostings can be especially tricky, though they are very tasty and quite impressive. Here are a few tips to help you along the path to perfect meringues.

Use a deep, narrow bowl, which makes the job easier by allowing for aeration, which is what a meringue is all about—it's simply aerated egg white, so don't let all of the following steps scare you. First, whip the egg whites for 1 to 2 minutes, until frothy and foamy, pushing the beater around in the bowl to incorporate air into the whites. The frothy egg white mixture contains bubbles and will be cloudy, not clear. Continue whipping, and in another 30 seconds or so, you will arrive at the *soft-peak stage.* You know you are at the soft-peak stage when you lift the whisk or beater out of the bowl of egg whites, and a little bit of the mixture attempts to cling to the utensil and then sinks back down gently, forming a peak that is folded over. The whites at this stage are denser than at the frothy stage. Once at the soft-peak stage, you will need to watch very carefully because the egg whites will go to the *stiff-peak stage* within 10 to 45 seconds. The indicator for this stage? When you lift your whisk out of the bowl, you are left with a peak that does not sink—it stands up straight. At this stage, the egg whites are very shiny; this is when it is time to whip in your agave nectar, which will turn the mixture from shiny to a glossy, almost glittery, luminescence. When making your meringue frostings, make *sure* that your egg whites are at the stiff-peak stage before whipping in any sweetener, or the frosting will not work and will collapse, looking very wet again. Whip very briefly to incorporate the sweetener and keep whipping until the peaks are stiff again. When you reach the stiff-peak stage again, stop so that you do not overwhip.

Another word to the wise: overwhipping can be as problematic as underwhipping your egg whites. Going beyond the stiff-peak stage will result in a dry, grainy-looking mixture with limp peaks. If this happens, it is time to get out new eggs and start over. I've made meringues instinctively for as long as I can remember; it is explaining this technique to others that I find challenging. I am grateful to Melissa Gray of NPR and *All Cakes Considered* fame who has a lovely description in her wonderful book of how to make stiff egg whites that guided me in writing my own brief egg white tutorial.

INGREDIENTS

As in my previous book, *The Gluten-Free Almond Flour Cookbook*, almond flour plays an essential role in the recipes here. The co-star this time around? Coconut flour. In fact, the majority of the recipes in this book feature coconut flour. While I definitely prefer almond flour for certain dishes, such as cookies, and I also find it excellent when used as a coating (for "breading" chicken and fish), I am partial to coconut flour when it comes to making light and fluffy cakes.

Many of my recipes are very brand specific. This is because the ingredients that I use are so new that there is a great variation from brand to brand and industry standards have not yet been developed for many of these ingredients. Therefore, when I specify a brand, it is important to use it to get the intended results.

Agave Nectar

Agave nectar is my sweetener of choice. It has a smooth, neutral flavor and keeps baked goods moist. Although I have written an entire cookbook of desserts, I do believe that anything made with any kind of sweetener other than fruit (or stevia) is best saved for special occasions. If agave nectar does not work for you, feel free to experiment with the likes of honey, brown rice syrup, xylitol, or fruit purees.

Arrowroot Powder

I use arrowroot in two ways in this book. First, it is used in many of the cupcake recipes as an adjunct to almond and/or coconut flour. Second, I sometimes use it as a thickener in vegan frostings.

Blanched Almond Flour

Almond flour is made from blanched almonds that are ground into a flour. All of the recipes in this book call for almond flour, not almond meal—they will not work with almond meal, which is a coarser product and contains almonds that are not blanched. Almond flour is very high in protein and low in carbohydrates.

You can find blanched almond flour in most health-food stores; however, I purchase mine online because it is generally of higher quality and significantly cheaper than what I find in stores. A note on Bob's Red Mill almond flour: I have found that this product does not work in my recipes.

Butter Substitute

I have found Earth Balance Natural Buttery Spread (Soy Free) to be a delicious, gluten-free, dairy-free butter substitute. It is an indispensable ingredient when it comes to creating vegan frostings. My children like to smother their (gluten-free) toast with it, and I enjoy its rich, buttery flavor on just about anything. Be sure not to switch brands in the recipes that call for this ingredient because other products likely will not yield the desired results.

Chia Seeds

Chia seeds are one of the only vegetarian sources of omega-3s. I use ground chia seeds in Vegan Chocolate Cupcakes (page 23) as a binder to hold together this egg-free batter. I store chia seeds and chia seed meal in a glass jar in the freezer for optimum freshness.

Chocolate

I use organic unsweetened cocoa powder in these recipes. When a recipe calls for dark chocolate chips, I use organic dark chocolate chips that are 73 percent cacao. While changing types of chocolate chips (and percentages of cacao) won't matter in the cupcake recipes where the chips are studded throughout a batter, it is critical for frosting recipes that the specified type of chocolate be used—be sure to use dark chocolate (73 percent cacao).

Semisweet chocolate chips are not used all that frequently in this book; however, it's a nice ingredient to keep around, and my children like to munch on them by the handful. I use 365 Organic Semi-Sweet Chocolate Chips, which you can find at Whole Foods.

I like to use mini chocolate chips in cupcakes as well as for a garnish, the way sprinkles are used. They're quite fun and festive and add a nice extra hit of chocolate. I use gluten-free mini chocolate chips from Enjoy Life.

White chocolate is cocoa butter without the cacao. When a recipe calls for white chocolate chips, I use Sunspire brand, which does contain dairy.

Coconut Flour

Coconut flour is fabulous for baking cakes and cupcakes. Recipes that use it rise quite nicely and are light and fluffy. Many people think that a coconut-flavored dessert will result from a recipe that uses this flour. In my experience, this is not the case. Coconut flour sucks up moisture and requires a tremendous amount of liquid. In recipes calling for coconut flour, the ratio of wet ingredients to dry is literally off the charts.

Everything I know about coconut flour, I learned from Bruce Fife's fantastic book, *Cooking with Coconut Flour*. He is the master when it comes to this flour, which is made from finely ground, dried, and defatted coconut. It is high in fiber and low in carbohydrates. Another benefit? It is much cheaper than almond flour.

Coconut Milk

I use Thai Kitchen organic coconut milk in these recipes. It is essential to purchase this brand for the Vegan Coconut Whip (page 94); the recipe will not work with other brands. Be sure to purchase the regular coconut milk, not the reduced-fat or "lite" version.

Coconut Oil

Coconut oil is an ingredient that imparts a strong coconut flavor to the recipes in which it is used. Primarily I use it in recipes such as Coconut Cupcakes (page 52) and Vegan Coconut Frosting (page 97). While the traditional medical community frowns upon coconut oil because of its saturated fats, it is gaining favor in alternative health circles, especially among those who follow a paleo, or primal, eating style, believing it is good for hair and skin and may have anti-fungal properties. Be sure to use virgin unrefined coconut oil in these recipes, store it at room temperature, and melt it over very low heat before using in the cupcake recipes (it's okay to add it while still warm to these recipes).

Eggs

I use organic large eggs in all of the recipes that call for eggs in this book. While the organic part is, of course, optional, use the recommended size (large) to ensure that your batters will turn into beautiful cupcakes.

Flax Meal

Ground flax meal is a powerhouse of compounds that are anti-inflammatory. In terms of taste, I add it to breads and muffins to give a strong, "whole grain" nutty flavor. I store flax seeds and flax meal in the freezer to keep them fresh.

Food Coloring

In all of the cupcake and frosting recipes that call for food coloring, I use a product made from natural vegetable dyes called India Tree Natural Decorating Colors. I do not like to use artificial dyes because some studies haven shown these to be less than healthy in a variety of ways. Stick to natural food dyes for your children, and yourself.

Fruit Spread

I adore Rigoni di Asiago fruit spread because it is made from organic fruits and naturally sweetened with fruit juices; all of the flavors are delicious.

Grapeseed Oil

I use grapeseed oil in place of butter in my recipes. It has a rich and smooth, buttery flavor, and using a dairy-free ingredient as the fat in my recipes makes them accessible to more people with different food intolerances. I purchase my oils in glass bottles and store them in a cool place for no more than 6 months. Like many oils, grapeseed oil can turn rancid if kept for longer.

Ice Cream Cones

I use the gluten-free wafer cones from Let's Do brand. Buy the flat-bottomed version.

Salt

I use finely ground sea salt in my dessert recipes. The fact that it is finely ground is key—you do not want little boulders of salt in your cupcakes. Sea salt is also important in these recipes—if you use a different type, the results might be a tad salty.

Shortening

I use Spectrum Organic All Vegetable Shortening in my Vegan Butter-cream recipe (page 95); it is made of organic palm oil. Making frosting without butter and sugar is a bit of a challenge, but this shortening makes it easier and the results are quite delicious.

Sprinkles

Thank goodness for organic, gluten-free sprinkles. Obviously, they offer no health benefits; however, they sure do add some fun to a cupcake. My children enjoy being able to have sprinkles, just like their friends who can eat gluten. I use Let's Do brand gluten-free sprinkles.

Stevia

Stevia is an excellent herbal sweetener. The trick with stevia is finding a brand that does not have a strong aftertaste. I use Sweet Leaf brand stevia in liquid form.

Vanilla Extract

I use a high-quality, organic, gluten-free vanilla extract made by Flavorganics.

Yacon Syrup

Yacon is a root composed primarily of water and fructo-oligosaccharides (FOS). These types of short-chain sugars have a lower caloric value (because they are digested anaerobically) and a high fiber content. This sweetener imparts a lovely molasses-like flavor to baked goods such as Ginger "Molasses" Cupcakes (page 65).

CLASSIC CUPCAKES

Vanilla Cupcakes ❀ 20

Chocolate Cupcakes ❀ 22

Vegan Chocolate Cupcakes ❀ 23

Strawberry Cupcakes ❀ 24

Marble Cupcakes ❀ 27

Red Velvet Cupcakes ❀ 28

Chocolate Chip Mini Cupcakes ❀ 30

Vanilla Cupcakes

MAKES 9 ❊ SWEETNESS: MEDIUM

These are my go-to cupcake because they're great with any frosting; try them with my Cream Cheese Frosting (page 95), Vegan Chocolate Frosting (page 92), or one of your own creations.

½ cup plus 2 tablespoons coconut flour
½ teaspoon sea salt
¼ teaspoon baking soda
4 large eggs
⅓ cup grapeseed oil
½ cup agave nectar
1 tablespoon vanilla extract

Preheat the oven to 350°F. Line 9 muffin cups with paper liners.

In a large bowl, combine the coconut flour, salt, and baking soda. In a medium bowl, whisk together the eggs, grapeseed oil, agave nectar, and vanilla extract. Blend the wet ingredients into the coconut flour mixture with a handheld mixer until thoroughly combined.

Scoop ¼ cup of batter into each prepared muffin cup.

Bake for 18 to 22 minutes, until a toothpick inserted into the center of a cupcake comes out with just a few moist crumbs attached. Let the cupcakes cool in the pan for 1 hour, then frost and serve.

Vanilla Cupcakes with Vegan Chocolate Frosting (page 92) and Chocolate Cupcakes (page 22) with White Chocolate Frosting (page 94)

Chocolate Cupcakes

MAKES 9 ❖ SWEETNESS: MEDIUM

Smother these little treats with my White Chocolate Frosting (page 94) or try them with Vegan Chocolate Frosting (page 92), sprinkled with Chocolate Dirt (page 98). Chocolate lovers unite! *Pictured on page 21.*

$1/4$ cup coconut flour
$1/4$ cup unsweetened cocoa powder
$1/4$ teaspoon sea salt
$1/2$ teaspoon baking soda
4 large eggs
$1/4$ cup grapeseed oil
$1/2$ cup agave nectar

Preheat the oven to 350°F. Line 9 muffin cups with paper liners.

In a large bowl, combine the coconut flour, cocoa powder, salt, and baking soda. In a medium bowl, whisk together the eggs, grapeseed oil, and agave nectar. Blend the wet ingredients into the coconut flour mixture with a handheld mixer until thoroughly combined.

Scoop $1/4$ cup of batter into each prepared muffin cup.

Bake for 18 to 22 minutes, until a toothpick inserted into the center of a cupcake comes out with just a few moist crumbs attached. Let the cupcakes cool in the pan for 1 hour, then frost and serve.

Vegan Chocolate Cupcakes

MAKES 9 ✢ SWEETNESS: MEDIUM

When you want to share sweets with vegan friends and family, use this recipe as a substitute for those in the Special Occasion section. These cupcakes are not only gluten free, they are also made without dairy or eggs—not an easy feat. Make your own delicious creation by pairing them with Vegan Buttercream (page 95), Vegan Chocolate Frosting (page 92), or Vegan Coconut Whip (page 94). Thanks to Ali Segersten from wholelifenutrition.net for giving me a head start on this recipe.

$1^1/_2$ cups blanched almond flour

$1/_4$ cup unsweetened cocoa powder

1 tablespoon arrowroot powder

1 tablespoon ground chia seeds

1 tablespoon flax meal

$1/_4$ teaspoon sea salt

$1/_2$ teaspoon baking soda

$1/_4$ cup plus 2 tablespoons coconut milk

$1/_4$ cup plus 3 tablespoons agave nectar

1 tablespoon apple cider vinegar

1 tablespoon vanilla extract

Preheat the oven to 350°F. Line 9 muffin cups with paper liners.

In a large bowl, combine the almond flour, cocoa powder, arrowroot powder, ground chia seeds, flax meal, salt, and baking soda. In a medium bowl, whisk together the coconut milk, agave nectar, vinegar, and vanilla extract. Stir the wet ingredients into the almond flour mixture with a large spoon until thoroughly combined.

Scoop $^1/_4$ cup of batter into each prepared muffin cup.

Bake for 25 to 30 minutes, until a toothpick inserted into the center of a cupcake comes out with just a few moist crumbs attached. Let the cupcakes cool in the pan for 1 hour, then frost and serve.

Strawberry Cupcakes

MAKES 8 ❧ SWEETNESS: MEDIUM

My younger son loves these cupcakes and calls them Strawberry Spongecakes. He enjoys topping them with Cream Cheese Frosting (page 95), though they also pair quite nicely with Strawberry Meringue Frosting (page 97; pictured opposite). These pink-flecked pleasers are best made at the height of strawberry season.

1/2 cup coconut flour

1 tablespoon arrowroot powder

1/4 teaspoon sea salt

1/2 teaspoon baking soda

4 large eggs

1/2 cup agave nectar

1 tablespoon vanilla extract

1/2 cup finely chopped fresh strawberries

Preheat the oven to 350°F. Line 8 muffin cups with paper liners.

In a large bowl, combine the coconut flour, arrowroot powder, salt, and baking soda. In a medium bowl, whisk together the eggs, agave nectar, and vanilla extract. Blend the wet ingredients into the coconut flour mixture with a handheld mixer until thoroughly combined, then fold in the strawberries.

Scoop 1/4 cup of batter into each prepared muffin cup.

Bake for 20 to 25 minutes, until a toothpick inserted into the center of a cupcake comes out with just a few moist crumbs attached. Let the cupcakes cool in the pan for 1 hour, then frost and serve.

Marble Cupcakes

MAKES 8 ❈ SWEETNESS: MEDIUM

An aesthetic wonder, these cupcakes might be a little more work to make than some; however, the swirled result is worth every bit of extra effort. My older son loves these with Vegan Chocolate Frosting (page 92), while my younger son likes them without any frosting at all. Conclusion? They're darn good.

VANILLA BATTER

1/4 cup coconut flour
1/4 teaspoon baking soda
2 large eggs
2 tablespoons grapeseed oil
1/3 cup agave nectar

CHOCOLATE BATTER

2 tablespoons coconut flour
2 tablespoons unsweetened cocoa powder
1/2 teaspoon baking soda
2 large eggs
1 tablespoon grapeseed oil
1/4 cup agave nectar

❈

Preheat the oven to 350°F. Line 8 muffin cups with paper liners.

To make the vanilla batter, in a large bowl, combine the coconut flour and baking soda. In a medium bowl, whisk together the eggs, grapeseed oil, and agave nectar. Stir the wet ingredients into the coconut flour mixture with a large spoon until thoroughly combined.

To make the chocolate batter, in a large bowl, combine the coconut flour, cocoa powder, and baking soda. In a medium bowl, whisk together the eggs, grapeseed oil, and agave nectar. Stir the wet ingredients into the coconut flour mixture with a large spoon until thoroughly combined.

Fill each prepared muffin cup with 4 tablespoons of batter, alternating tablespoons of chocolate and vanilla, starting with chocolate batter and ending with vanilla. Use a toothpick to swirl the batter in figure eights.

Bake for 18 to 22 minutes, until a toothpick inserted into the center of a cupcake comes out with just a few moist crumbs attached. Let the cupcakes cool in the pan for 1 hour, then frost and serve.

Red Velvet Cupcakes

MAKES 9 ❖ SWEETNESS: MEDIUM

Everybody loves the classic, yet intriguing red velvet cupcake with Cream Cheese Frosting (page 95). Enjoy my version made with natural vegetable coloring instead of the scary artificial red dye normally found in the traditional recipe.

1/2 cup coconut flour

2 tablespoons unsweetened cocoa powder

1/4 teaspoon sea salt

1/4 teaspoon baking soda

4 large eggs

2 tablespoons grapeseed oil

1/2 cup agave nectar

1 tablespoon red food coloring, made from vegetable dye

Preheat the oven to 350°F. Line 9 muffin cups with paper liners.

In a large bowl, combine the coconut flour, cocoa powder, salt, and baking soda. In a medium bowl, whisk together the eggs, grapeseed oil, agave nectar, and food coloring. Blend the wet ingredients into the coconut flour mixture with a handheld mixer until thoroughly combined.

Scoop 1/4 cup of batter into each prepared muffin cup.

Bake for 18 to 22 minutes, until a toothpick inserted into the center of a cupcake comes out with just a few moist crumbs attached. Let the cupcakes cool in the pan for 1 hour, then frost and serve.

Chocolate Chip Mini Cupcakes

MAKES 36 MINI CUPCAKES ⊰⊱ SWEETNESS: MEDIUM

These bite-size, grab-and-go mini chip–studded gems are a taste sensation at children's birthday parties. Or, if you're hesitant to commit to a regular-size cupcake, a mini such as this might be the perfect solution. Enjoy!

1/2 cup coconut flour
1/2 cup blanched almond flour
1/4 teaspoon sea salt
1 teaspoon baking soda
3 large eggs
1/4 cup grapeseed oil
1/2 cup agave nectar
1/2 cup mini chocolate chips (semisweet)

Preheat the oven to 350°F. Grease a mini-muffin pan generously with grapeseed oil.

In a large bowl, combine the coconut flour, almond flour, salt, and baking soda. In a medium bowl, whisk together the eggs, grapeseed oil, and agave nectar. Blend the wet ingredients into the coconut flour mixture with a handheld mixer until thoroughly combined, then stir in the mini chocolate chips.

Scoop 1 tablespoon of batter into each prepared muffin cup.

Bake for 6 to 9 minutes, until a toothpick inserted into the center of a cupcake comes out with a few moist crumbs attached. Let the cupcakes cool in the pan for 1 hour, then serve.

CHOCOLATE CUPCAKES

Triple Chocolate Cupcakes

MAKES 9 ❧ SWEETNESS: HIGH

Dark, milk, and white chocolate chips are sprinkled throughout this rich chocolate cupcake. For a more sophisticated version, use only dark chocolate chips. Guaranteed to fulfill your daily chocolate craving.

1/4 cup coconut flour
1/4 cup unsweetened cocoa powder
1/4 teaspoon sea salt
1/4 teaspoon baking soda
3 large eggs
1/2 cup agave nectar
1/4 cup dark chocolate chips (73% cacao)
1/4 cup semisweet chocolate chips
1/4 cup white chocolate chips

Preheat the oven to 350°F. Line 9 muffin cups with paper liners.

In a large bowl, combine the coconut flour, cocoa powder, salt, and baking soda. In a medium bowl, whisk together the eggs and agave nectar. Blend the wet ingredients into the coconut flour mixture with a handheld mixer until thoroughly combined, then fold in all of the chocolate chips.

Scoop 1/4 cup of batter into each prepared muffin cup.

Bake for 25 to 30 minutes, until a toothpick inserted into the center of a cupcake comes out with just a few moist crumbs attached. Let the cupcakes cool in the pan for 1 hour, then serve.

Mocha Chip Cupcakes

MAKES 8 ❧ SWEETNESS: HIGH

Moist mocha cakes with dark chocolate chips, these nutritious yet decadent sweets are equally well suited for a post-workout snack or for a party with Vegan Chocolate Frosting (page 92).

1/4 cup coconut flour

1/4 cup unsweetened cocoa powder

2 tablespoons decaf espresso beans, finely ground

1/4 teaspoon sea salt

1/4 teaspoon baking soda

2 large eggs

1/2 cup agave nectar

1/2 cup dark chocolate chips (73% cacao)

Preheat the oven to 350°F. Line 8 muffin cups with paper liners.

In a large bowl, combine the coconut flour, cocoa powder, ground espresso, salt, and baking soda. In a medium bowl, whisk together the eggs and agave nectar. Blend the wet ingredients into the coconut flour mixture with a handheld mixer until thoroughly combined, then stir in the chocolate chips.

Scoop 1/4 cup of batter into each prepared muffin cup.

Bake for 23 to 28 minutes, until a toothpick inserted into the center of a cupcake comes out with just a few moist crumbs attached. Let the cupcakes cool in the pan for 1 hour, then frost and serve.

Chocolate Peanut Butter Cupcakes

MAKES 9 ✌ SWEETNESS: MEDIUM

What better way to savor peanut butter and chocolate than with this dense, rich confection? They're like Reese's peanut butter cups in cupcake form—perfect for kids of all ages. Top with Chocolate Ganache (page 92).

BATTER
$1/2$ cup blanched almond flour
$1/4$ cup coconut flour
$1/4$ cup unsweetened cocoa powder
$1/4$ teaspoon sea salt
$1/2$ teaspoon baking soda
4 large eggs
2 tablespoons grapeseed oil
$1/2$ cup agave nectar

FILLING
$1/2$ cup creamy roasted peanut butter
$1/4$ cup agave nectar
1 teaspoon vanilla extract
$1/2$ teaspoon sea salt

Preheat the oven to 350°F. Line 9 muffin cups with paper liners.

To make the batter, in a large bowl, combine the almond flour, coconut flour, cocoa powder, salt, and baking soda. In a medium bowl, whisk together the eggs, grapeseed oil, and agave nectar. Blend the wet ingredients into the almond flour mixture with a handheld mixer until thoroughly combined.

To make the filling, in a medium bowl, combine the peanut butter, agave nectar, vanilla extract, and salt and mash together with a fork until smooth.

Scoop 1 tablespoon of the filling into each prepared muffin cup, then cover with $1/4$ cup of batter.

Bake for 20 to 24 minutes, until a toothpick inserted $1/2$ inch from the edge of the cupcake (to avoid the peanut butter center) comes out with just a few moist crumbs attached. Let the cupcakes cool in the pan for 1 hour, then frost and serve.

Cookie Surprise Cupcakes

MAKES 10 ❁ SWEETNESS: MEDIUM

When I met Robyn Baldwin, one of my loyal readers, at a book signing in Davis, California (my hometown), she gave me the idea for these chocolate cupcakes with a cookie center. Thanks, Robyn! Frost with Vegan Chocolate Frosting (page 92).

BATTER
5 tablespoons coconut flour
1/4 cup unsweetened cocoa powder
1/4 teaspoon sea salt
1/2 teaspoon baking soda
4 large eggs
1/2 cup agave nectar

COOKIE DOUGH
2/3 cup blanched almond flour
1/4 teaspoon baking soda
3 tablespoons agave nectar
5 tablespoons mini chocolate chips (semisweet)

Preheat the oven to 350°F. Line 10 muffin cups with paper liners.

To make the batter, in a large bowl, combine the coconut flour, cocoa powder, salt, and baking soda. In a medium bowl, whisk together the eggs and agave nectar. Blend the wet ingredients into the coconut flour mixture with a handheld mixer until thoroughly combined.

To make the cookie dough, in a large bowl, combine the almond flour and baking soda. Stir the agave nectar into the almond flour mixture until thoroughly combined, then fold in the mini chocolate chips.

Scoop out 1 tablespoon of cookie dough, roll into a ball, and place in each prepared muffin cup, then cover with 3 tablespoons of batter.

Bake for 18 to 22 minutes, until a toothpick inserted into the center of a cupcake comes out with just a few moist crumbs attached. Let the cupcakes cool in the pan for 3 hours in order to give the filling a chance to set up, then frost and serve.

Chocolate Banana Cupcakes

MAKES 12 ❧ SWEETNESS: MEDIUM

**Chocolate and banana is one of my favorite flavor combinations.
Try these cupcakes with Banana Whipped Cream Frosting (page 93),
along with a side of strawberries.**

1/2 cup coconut flour
1/4 cup unsweetened cocoa powder
1/4 teaspoon sea salt
1/2 teaspoon baking soda
4 large eggs
1/2 cup agave nectar
1 cup (2 to 3) mashed very ripe bananas

Preheat the oven to 350°F. Line 12 muffin cups with paper liners.

In a large bowl, combine the coconut flour, cocoa powder, salt, and baking soda. In a medium bowl, whisk together the eggs and agave nectar. Stir the wet ingredients into the coconut flour mixture with a large spoon until thoroughly combined, then fold in the bananas.

Scoop 1/4 cup of batter into each prepared muffin cup.

Bake for 18 to 22 minutes, until a toothpick inserted into the center of a cupcake comes out with just a few moist crumbs attached. Let the cupcakes cool in the pan for 1 hour, then frost and serve.

Almond Fudge Cupcakes

MAKES 12 ❧ SWEETNESS: MEDIUM

Chocolate and almonds are a match made in heaven's kitchen. This cupcake has both healthy dark chocolate and antioxidant-rich almonds (a superfood) in a fudgy base for a little hit of healthy deliciousness in every bite. Try these with Chocolate Ganache (page 92).

1 cup blanched almond flour

2 tablespoons coconut flour

2 tablespoons unsweetened cocoa powder

1/4 teaspoon sea salt

1 teaspoon baking soda

4 large eggs

1/2 cup agave nectar

1 tablespoon almond extract

1/2 cup dark chocolate chips (73% cacao)

1/2 cup blanched slivered almonds

Preheat the oven to 350°F. Line 12 muffin cups with paper liners.

In a large bowl, combine the almond flour, coconut flour, cocoa powder, salt, and baking soda. In a medium bowl, whisk together the eggs, agave nectar, and almond extract. Blend the wet ingredients into the almond flour mixture with a handheld mixer until thoroughly combined, then stir in the chocolate chips and almonds.

Scoop 1/4 cup of batter into each prepared muffin cup.

Bake for 15 to 20 minutes, until a toothpick inserted into the center of a cupcake comes out with just a few moist crumbs attached. Let the cupcakes cool in the pan for 1 hour, then frost and serve.

Fallen Chocolate Soufflé Cupcakes

MAKES 12 ❀ SWEETNESS: HIGH

This gooey cupcake oozes chocolate goodness. These are not your regular cupcakes—they will look like a little chocolate bowl with a crater in the middle—perfect for rich fillings! Serve warm, filled with a big dollop of Whipped Cream Frosting (page 93), and eat them with a spoon.

1¹/₂ cups blanched almond flour
¹/₄ cup unsweetened cocoa powder
¹/₄ teaspoon sea salt
¹/₄ teaspoon baking soda
2 large eggs
1 cup agave nectar
1 tablespoon vanilla extract
1 cup dark chocolate chips (73% cacao)

❀

Preheat the oven to 350°F. Line 12 muffin cups with paper liners.

In a large bowl, combine the almond flour, cocoa powder, salt, and baking soda. In a medium bowl, whisk together the eggs, agave nectar, and vanilla extract. Blend the wet ingredients into the almond flour mixture with a handheld mixer until thoroughly combined, then stir in the chocolate chips.

Scoop ¹/₄ cup of batter into each prepared muffin cup.

Bake for 18 to 22 minutes, until the center of each cupcake is puffy and the edges are drier and darker than the center. The cupcakes will fall when removed from the oven and the centers will be gooey, even when fully baked.

Let the cupcakes cool in the pan for 10 minutes. The tops of the cupcakes may have overflowed while baking; if this happens, loosen the edges of the tops with a butter knife, and use the butter knife to gently lever the cupcakes out of the pan. Serve warm.

White Chocolate Cherry Cupcakes

This cupcake with white chocolate chips and chunks of cherry is superb with White Chocolate Frosting (page 94). Top the cupcakes with a cherry for a special finishing touch. For a holiday version, substitute frozen cranberries for the cherries in the batter.

¹/₂ cup coconut flour
2 tablespoons arrowroot powder
¹/₄ teaspoon sea salt
1 teaspoon baking soda
4 eggs
¹/₂ cup agave nectar
¹/₂ cup frozen cherries, cut into quarters
1 cup white chocolate chips

Preheat the oven to 350°F. Line 11 muffin cups with paper liners.

In a large bowl, combine the coconut flour, arrowroot powder, salt, and baking soda; set aside 1 tablespoon of this coconut flour mixture. In a medium bowl, whisk together the eggs and agave nectar. Blend the wet ingredients into the coconut flour mixture with a handheld mixer until thoroughly combined.

Sprinkle the reserved tablespoon of coconut flour mixture over the cherries, tossing to coat thoroughly. Fold the cherries and white chocolate chips into the batter.

Scoop ¹/₄ cup of batter into each prepared muffin cup.

Bake for 20 to 25 minutes, until a toothpick inserted into the center of a cupcake comes out with just a few moist crumbs attached. These cupcakes brown very quickly, but they are not done until they pass the toothpick test. Let the cupcakes cool in the pan for 1 hour, then frost and serve.

Flourless Chocolate Coconut Cupcakes

MAKES 8 ❊ SWEETNESS: MEDIUM

Have a soft spot for Mounds candy bars? This simple flourless cupcake is made of shredded coconut and chocolate. It's great with my
Vegan Chocolate Frosting (page 92) or without any frosting at all.
Shredded coconut provides great fiber, and the dark chocolate is full
of antioxidants.

1 cup dark chocolate chips (73% cacao)
1 cup unsweetened shredded coconut
3 large eggs
1/3 cup agave nectar
1/4 teaspoon sea salt

Preheat the oven to 350°F. Line 8 muffin cups with paper liners.

Place the chocolate chips in a food processor and pulse until it has the consistency of coarse sand. Add the coconut and pulse briefly until combined, about 10 seconds, then add the eggs, agave nectar, and salt and pulse until well combined, 10 to 15 seconds.

Scoop 1/4 cup of batter into each prepared muffin cup.

Bake for 20 to 25 minutes, until a toothpick inserted into the center of a cupcake comes out clean. Let the cupcakes cool in the pan for 1 hour, then frost and serve.

Flourless Chocolate Hazelnut Cupcakes

MAKES 10 ❊ SWEETNESS: LOW

Try this rich, dense, flourless cupcake recipe with Chocolate Ganache (page 92); enjoy with a nice strong cup of coffee or tea.

1¹/₂ cups dark chocolate chips (73% cacao)

1 cup hazelnuts

3 large eggs

¹/₄ cup agave nectar

1 tablespoon vanilla extract

¹/₄ teaspoon sea salt

Preheat the oven to 350°F. Line 10 muffin cups with paper liners.

Combine the chocolate chips and hazelnuts in a food processor and process until they have the consistency of coarse sand. Add the eggs and agave nectar and pulse until combined, about 10 seconds, then add the vanilla extract and salt and pulse again until combined, another 10 seconds.

Scoop ¹/₄ cup of batter into each prepared muffin cup.

Bake for 20 to 25 minutes, until a toothpick inserted into the center of a cupcake comes out clean. Let the cupcakes cool in the pan for 1 hour, then frost and serve.

Flourless White Chocolate Cupcakes

MAKES 12 ⊰⊱ SWEETNESS: HIGH

Who could guess that this heavenly confection is made with a mere three ingredients? The result: a rich smooth cupcake with a wonderfully crispy top, quick and easy enough to make for a weeknight dessert. Enjoy these cupcakes plain, or for a super sugar high, top with White Chocolate Frosting (page 94).

1½ cups white chocolate chips
1¼ cups blanched slivered almonds
3 large eggs

Preheat the oven to 350°F. Line 12 muffin cups with paper liners.

Place the white chocolate chips and almonds in a food processor and process until they have the consistency of coarse sand. Add the eggs and pulse until combined, about 10 seconds.

Scoop a scant ¼ cup of batter into each prepared muffin cup.

Bake for 18 to 22 minutes, until a toothpick inserted into the center of a cupcake comes out clean and the edges of the cupcakes are golden. Let the cupcakes cool in the pan for 1 hour, then frost and serve.

FRUITY CUPCAKES

Blueberry Lemon Cupcakes

MAKES 12 ❧ SWEETNESS: MEDIUM

Light and zesty, these cupcakes are excellent with lemon cream cheese frosting (see page 96; pictured opposite) or Whipped Cream Frosting (page 93). Pair with a frittata or quiche for a memorable Mother's Day brunch.

1/2 cup coconut flour

1/4 teaspoon sea salt

1/4 teaspoon baking soda

4 large eggs

1/2 cup grapeseed oil

1/2 cup agave nectar

2 tablespoons firmly packed lemon zest (2 to 3 lemons)

1 cup frozen blueberries

Preheat the oven to 350°F. Line 12 muffin cups with paper liners.

In a large bowl, combine the coconut flour, salt, and baking soda. In a medium bowl, whisk together the eggs, grapeseed oil, agave nectar, and lemon zest. Blend the wet ingredients into the coconut flour mixture with a handheld mixer until thoroughly combined, then fold in the blueberries.

Scoop 1/4 cup of batter into each prepared muffin cup.

Bake for 22 to 26 minutes, until a toothpick inserted into the center of a cupcake comes out with just a few moist crumbs attached. Let the cupcakes cool in the pan for 1 hour, then frost and serve.

Cranberry Apricot Cupcakes

MAKES 10 ❧ SWEETNESS: HIGH

Dried cranberries provide vitamin C and dried apricots offer vitamin A in this fruit-filled cupcake. As a mom, I'm happy to see the boys pack this in their lunches. You can also serve it for dessert with Cream Cheese Frosting (page 95), another perfect example of healthy food that tastes great.

2 cups blanched almond flour
1/4 teaspoon sea salt
1/4 teaspoon baking soda
2 large eggs
1/2 cup agave nectar
1/2 cup dried cranberries
1/4 cup dried apricots, quartered

Preheat the oven to 350°F. Line 10 muffin cups with paper liners.

In a large bowl, combine the almond flour, salt, and baking soda. In a medium bowl, whisk together the eggs and agave nectar. Stir the wet ingredients into the almond flour mixture with a large spoon until thoroughly combined, then fold in the cranberries and apricots.

Scoop 1/4 cup of batter into each prepared muffin cup.

Bake for 18 to 22 minutes, until a toothpick inserted into the center of a cupcake comes out with just a few moist crumbs attached. Let the cupcakes cool in the pan for 1 hour, then frost and serve.

Vanilla Fig Cupcakes

MAKES 10 ❖ SWEETNESS: MEDIUM

Speckled with vanilla beans and dried figs, these light and delicate cupcakes make a sophisticated end to a lovely meal, or a satisfying accompaniment to afternoon tea. Try these plain or with Vegan Buttercream (page 95).

1/2 cup coconut flour
1/2 teaspoon sea salt
1/4 teaspoon baking soda
4 large eggs
1/2 cup grapeseed oil
1/2 cup agave nectar
1 vanilla bean pod, split lengthwise
1 cup dried figs, finely chopped

Preheat the oven to 350°F. Line 10 muffin cups with paper liners.

In a large bowl, combine the coconut flour, salt, and baking soda. In a medium bowl, whisk together the eggs, grapeseed oil, and agave nectar. Scrape the tiny vanilla beans (they look like seeds) out of the pod into the wet mixture. Blend the wet ingredients into the coconut flour mixture with a handheld mixer until thoroughly combined, then fold in the figs.

Scoop 1/4 cup of batter into each prepared muffin cup.

Bake for 18 to 22 minutes, until a toothpick inserted into the center of a cupcake comes out with just a few moist crumbs attached. Let the cupcakes cool in the pan for 1 hour, then frost and serve.

Raspberry Cheesecake Cupcakes

MAKES 12 ⋇ SWEETNESS: MEDIUM

Made with goat cheese and raspberry jam, these healthy yet decadent mini cheesecakes are scrumptiously satisfying. Take note that they puff when baked and settle as they cool. Try experimenting with different flavors of jam, such as orange, cherry, or apricot. This is my boys' favorite dessert and they ask me to make it quite often.

CRUST

1 cup pecans

5 dates, pitted

1 tablespoon grapeseed oil

1/4 teaspoon sea salt

TOPPING

8 ounces goat cheese

3 large eggs

1/3 cup agave nectar

1 tablespoon vanilla extract

1/4 cup raspberry fruit spread

⋇

Preheat the oven to 350°F. Line 12 muffin cups with paper liners.

To make the crust, combine the pecans and dates in a food processor and pulse until coarsely ground. Pulse in the grapeseed oil and salt. Spoon 1 tablespoon of the crust mixture into each prepared muffin cup. Using your fingers, press down to flatten the crust.

Rinse out and dry the food processor. To make the topping, combine the goat cheese, eggs, agave nectar, and vanilla extract in the food processor and process for 60 seconds, or until smooth.

Scoop 3 tablespoons of topping into each prepared muffin cup, then top each with 1 teaspoon of fruit spread.

Bake for 24 to 28 minutes, until the edges of the mini cheesecakes are lightly golden. Let the cupcakes cool in the pan for 1 hour, then serve.

Piña Colada Cupcakes

MAKES 10 ❖ SWEETNESS: HIGH

Pineapple, coconut, and white chocolate chips bring the flavor of the tropics into your home, even in the depths of winter. I like them plain or topped with Vegan Coconut Frosting (page 97). School bake sale? Try these super-sweet treats for a sure sellout.

1/2 cup coconut flour
1/2 teaspoon sea salt
1 teaspoon baking soda
4 large eggs
1/2 cup coconut oil, melted over very low heat
1/2 cup agave nectar
1/2 cup unsweetened shredded coconut
1/2 cup dried pineapple, finely chopped
1 cup white chocolate chips

Preheat the oven to 350°F. Line 10 muffin cups with paper liners.

In a large bowl, combine the coconut flour, salt, and baking soda. In a medium bowl, whisk together the eggs, coconut oil, and agave nectar. Blend the wet ingredients into the coconut flour mixture with a handheld mixer until thoroughly combined, then stir in the shredded coconut, pineapple, and white chocolate chips.

Scoop 1/4 cup of batter into each prepared muffin cup.

Bake for 18 to 22 minutes, until a toothpick inserted into the center of a cupcake comes out with just a few moist crumbs attached. Let the cupcakes cool in the pan for 1 hour, then frost and serve.

Coconut Cupcakes

MAKES 9 ❀ SWEETNESS: MEDIUM

My favorite way to eat these cupcakes is smothered in Vegan Coconut Frosting (page 97), with a touch of toasted coconut flakes on top. To toast, preheat the oven to 350°F, and spread $1/2$ cup of coconut flakes in a thin layer on a parchment paper–lined baking sheet. Place in the oven for 2 to 3 minutes, until golden brown. Remove from the oven, let cool completely, and then scatter over frosted cupcakes for a triple coconut threat.

$1/2$ cup coconut flour
$1/4$ teaspoon sea salt
1 teaspoon baking soda
4 large eggs
$1/2$ cup coconut oil, melted over very low heat
$1/2$ cup agave nectar
1 tablespoon vanilla extract
$1/2$ cup unsweetened shredded coconut
1 cup coconut flakes, toasted

Preheat the oven to 350°F. Line 9 muffin cups with paper liners.

In a large bowl, combine the coconut flour, salt, and baking soda. In a medium bowl, whisk together the eggs, coconut oil, agave nectar, and vanilla extract. Blend the wet ingredients into the coconut flour mixture with a handheld mixer until thoroughly combined, then stir in the shredded coconut.

Scoop $1/4$ cup of batter into each prepared muffin cup.

Bake for 18 to 22 minutes, until a toothpick inserted into the center of a cupcake comes out with just a few moist crumbs attached. Let the cupcakes cool in the pan for 1 hour, then frost, sprinkle with the toasted coconut flakes, and serve.

Lime Cupcakes

MAKES 10 ❧ SWEETNESS: MEDIUM

I love these light and fluffy lime cupcakes topped with Vegan Coconut Frosting (page 97) and a little lime zest. For a special touch, toast 1/2 cup of shredded coconut and sprinkle it over the frosted cupcakes. Simple and refreshing, they're perfect for a summer picnic or potluck.

1/2 cup coconut flour
1/2 cup blanched almond flour
1/2 teaspoon sea salt
1/4 teaspoon baking soda
3 large eggs
1/2 cup grapeseed oil
1/2 cup agave nectar
2 tablespoons firmly packed lime zest, plus more to decorate (about 3 limes)

Preheat the oven to 350°F. Line 10 muffin cups with paper liners.

In a large bowl, combine the coconut flour, almond flour, salt, and baking soda. In a medium bowl, whisk together the eggs, grapeseed oil, agave nectar, and 2 tablespoons lime zest. Blend the wet ingredients into the coconut flour mixture with a handheld mixer until thoroughly combined.

Scoop 1/4 cup of batter into each prepared muffin cup.

Bake for 18 to 22 minutes, until a toothpick inserted into the center of a cupcake comes out with just a few moist crumbs attached. Let the cupcakes cool in the pan for 1 hour, then frost, sprinkle with the remaining lime zest, and serve.

Orange Rosemary Cupcakes

MAKES 11 ✢ SWEETNESS: MEDIUM

Healthy bioflavonoids in orange zest and nutritious antioxidants in rosemary make this nourishing delight the perfect complement to a late afternoon cup of chai.

1/2 cup coconut flour
1/2 cup blanched almond flour
1/2 teaspoon sea salt
1 teaspoon baking soda
4 large eggs
1/2 cup grapeseed oil
1/2 cup agave nectar
2 tablespoons firmly packed orange zest
1 tablespoon finely chopped fresh rosemary

Preheat the oven to 350°F. Line 11 muffin cups with paper liners.

In a large bowl, combine the coconut flour, almond flour, salt, and baking soda. In a medium bowl, whisk together the eggs, grapeseed oil, agave nectar, and orange zest. Blend the wet ingredients into the coconut flour mixture with a handheld mixer until thoroughly combined, then stir in the rosemary.

Scoop 1/4 cup of batter into each prepared muffin cup.

Bake for 18 to 22 minutes, until a toothpick inserted into the center of a cupcake comes out with just a few moist crumbs attached. Let the cupcakes cool in the pan for 1 hour, then serve.

WARM AND SPICED CUPCAKES

Cinnamon Crumb Cupcakes

MAKES 10 ⊰⊱ SWEETNESS: MEDIUM

Try these aromatic, child-pleasing, cinnamon-walnut cupcakes on a Sunday morning. The comforting scent wafting from your kitchen will wake up all of your little sleepyheads. I like to serve these bare, without frosting, because the top of this cupcake is a streusel delight.

BATTER

1 cup blanched almond flour
2 tablespoons coconut flour
1/4 teaspoon sea salt
1 teaspoon baking soda
2 large eggs
1/2 cup agave nectar
1 tablespoon vanilla extract

TOPPING

3/4 cup blanched almond flour
1/2 cup walnuts, coarsely chopped
2 tablespoons ground cinnamon
1/4 cup agave nectar

⊰⊱

Preheat the oven to 350°F. Line 10 muffin cups with paper liners.

To make the batter, in a large bowl, combine the almond flour, coconut flour, salt, and baking soda. In a medium bowl, whisk together the eggs, agave nectar, and vanilla extract. Blend the wet ingredients into the almond flour mixture with a hand-held mixer until thoroughly combined.

To make the topping, in a medium bowl, combine the almond flour, walnuts, and cinnamon, then stir in the agave nectar.

Scoop 3 tablespoons of batter into each prepared muffin cup, then crumble 1 heaping tablespoon of the topping mixture over each cupcake.

Bake for 18 to 22 minutes, until a toothpick inserted into the center of a cupcake comes out with just a few moist crumbs attached. Let the cupcakes cool in the pan for 1 hour, then serve.

Cinnamon Crumb Cupcake and
Apple Spice Cupcake (page 60) with Cream Cheese Frosting (page 95)

Apple Spice Cupcakes

MAKES 10 ❋ SWEETNESS: MEDIUM

Tart chunks of green apple and warming cinnamon make this healthy and delicious cupcake the ideal after-school snack. Pack, unfrosted, in a lunch box along with a small container of Cream Cheese Frosting (page 95) for a special school-lunch dessert. *Pictured on page 59.*

1/2 cup coconut flour
1 tablespoon arrowroot powder
1 teaspoon baking soda
1 tablespoon ground cinnamon
1/2 teaspoon ground nutmeg
4 large eggs
1/4 cup grapeseed oil
1/2 cup agave nectar
1/2 cup coarsely chopped green apple

Preheat the oven to 350°F. Line 10 muffin cups with paper liners.

In a large bowl, combine the coconut flour, arrowroot powder, baking soda, cinnamon, and nutmeg. In a medium bowl, whisk together the eggs, grapeseed oil, and agave nectar. Blend the wet ingredients into the coconut flour mixture with a hand-held mixer until thoroughly combined, then fold in the apples.

Scoop 1/4 cup of batter into each prepared muffin cup.

Bake for 18 to 23 minutes, until a toothpick inserted into the center of a cupcake comes out with just a few moist crumbs attached. Let the cupcakes cool in the pan for 1 hour, then frost and serve.

Zucchini Cupcakes

MAKES 8 ❖ SWEETNESS: MEDIUM

Cream Cheese Frosting (page 95) pairs naturally with these cupcakes. If you can't have dairy, try them with Vegan Coconut Whip (page 94), which accents their nutty flavor quite nicely. I make these cupcakes every August; they're a great way to deal with the massive influx of zucchini during peak harvest.

¹⁄₄ cup coconut flour
¹⁄₄ cup blanched almond flour
1 tablespoon arrowroot powder
¹⁄₄ teaspoon sea salt
¹⁄₄ teaspoon baking soda
¹⁄₄ teaspoon ground cinnamon
4 large eggs
¹⁄₂ cup agave nectar
1 cup grated zucchini
¹⁄₄ cup walnuts, chopped
¹⁄₄ cup currants

Preheat the oven to 350°F. Line 8 muffin cups with paper liners.

In a large bowl, combine the coconut flour, almond flour, arrowroot powder, salt, baking soda, and cinnamon. In a medium bowl, whisk together the eggs and agave nectar. Blend the wet ingredients into the coconut flour mixture with a handheld mixer until thoroughly combined, then stir in the zucchini, walnuts, and currants. The batter will be a bit thin.

Scoop ¹⁄₄ cup of the batter into each prepared muffin cup.

Bake for 20 to 25 minutes, until a toothpick inserted into the center of a cupcake comes out with just a few moist crumbs attached. Let the cupcakes cool in the pan for 1 hour, then frost and serve.

Pecan Pie Cupcakes

MAKES 11 ❖ SWEETNESS: MEDIUM

Deliciously cinnamon-y pecan cupcakes are a wonderfully warming treat on a chilly winter day. I like to have mine smothered in Cream Cheese Frosting (page 95) with a cup of dandelion root coffee (you can find the recipe on my website, elanaspantry.com). Garnish these cupcakes with a few chopped pecans.

1 cup blanched almond flour
2 tablespoons coconut flour
1/2 teaspoon baking soda
1 tablespoon ground cinnamon
3 large eggs
1/2 cup yacon syrup
1 tablespoon vanilla extract
1 cup pecans, coarsely chopped

Preheat the oven to 350°F. Line 11 muffin cups with paper liners.

In a large bowl, combine the almond flour, coconut flour, baking soda, and cinnamon. In a medium bowl, whisk together the eggs, yacon syrup, and vanilla extract. Blend the wet ingredients into the almond flour mixture with a handheld mixer until thoroughly combined, then stir in the pecans.

Scoop 1/4 cup of batter into each prepared muffin cup.

Bake for 15 to 20 minutes, until a toothpick inserted into the center of a cupcake comes out with just a few moist crumbs attached. Let the cupcakes cool in the pan for 1 hour, then frost and serve.

Pecan Pie Cupcake with Cream Cheese Frosting (page 95) and Pumpkin Cupcakes (page 64) with Whipped Cream Frosting (page 93)

Pumpkin Cupcakes

MAKES 12 ✂ SWEETNESS: MEDIUM

Fragrant and brimming with health-boosting nutrients, these little cakes are a scrumptious alternative to pumpkin pie at Thanksgiving dinner. Top with Whipped Cream Frosting (page 93). *Pictured on page 63.*

3/4- to 1-pound small sugar pumpkin, acorn squash, or butternut squash

1 cup blanched almond flour

1/4 cup coconut flour

2 tablespoons arrowroot powder

2 teaspoons baking soda

1 tablespoon ground cinnamon

1 teaspoon ground nutmeg

1 teaspoon ground ginger

1/2 teaspoon ground cloves

3 large eggs

1/4 cup grapeseed oil

1/2 cup agave nectar

1 tablespoon apple cider vinegar

✂

Preheat the oven to 350°F. Line 12 muffin cups with paper liners.

Fill the bottom of a baking dish with 1/4 inch water. Cut the pumpkin in half vertically, remove the seeds, and place cut side down in the baking dish. Roast for 45 to 55 minutes, until the pumpkin is soft when pierced with a fork. Allow the pumpkin to cool, scrape the flesh into a bowl, then measure out 1/2 cup.

In a large bowl, combine the almond flour, coconut flour, arrowroot powder, baking soda, cinnamon, nutmeg, ginger, and cloves. In a food processor, pulse together the eggs, grapeseed oil, agave nectar, vinegar, and pumpkin until well combined. Add the almond flour mixture and pulse until thoroughly combined, about 30 seconds.

Scoop 1/4 cup of batter into each prepared muffin cup.

Bake for 18 to 23 minutes, until a toothpick inserted into the center of a cupcake comes out with just a few moist crumbs attached. Let the cupcakes cool in the pan for 1 hour, then frost and serve.

Ginger "Molasses" Cupcakes

MAKES 10 ❊ SWEETNESS: MEDIUM

Here's a fabulous cupcake to have on hand for the Thanksgiving and Christmas holidays. For extra zing, add 1 tablespoon fresh peeled and minced ginger to the batter (in addition to the ground ginger). I use low-glycemic yacon syrup in place of molasses in this recipe. Top with Cream Cheese Frosting (page 95).

1/2 cup coconut flour
1/4 teaspoon baking soda
1 tablespoon ground ginger
4 large eggs
1/2 cup grapeseed oil
1/2 cup yacon syrup

Preheat the oven to 350°F. Line 10 muffin cups with paper liners.

In a large bowl, combine the coconut flour, baking soda, and ginger. In a medium bowl, whisk together the eggs, grapeseed oil, and yacon syrup. Blend the wet ingredients into the coconut flour mixture with a handheld mixer until thoroughly combined.

Scoop 1/4 cup of batter into each prepared muffin cup.

Bake for 18 to 22 minutes, until a toothpick inserted into the center of a cupcake comes out with just a few moist crumbs attached. Let the cupcakes cool in the pan for 1 hour, then frost and serve.

Honey Walnut Cupcakes

MAKES 8 ❧ SWEETNESS: LOW

I wanted to include a recipe featuring honey in this book, because it is a unique flavor as much as a wonderful sweetener. Make sure the honey you use is pourable, with a fluid consistency—this will result in a moist cupcake, delicious both plain or smothered in Cream Cheese Frosting (page 95).

1¼ cups blanched almond flour
1 tablespoon coconut flour
¼ teaspoon sea salt
1 teaspoon baking soda
2 large eggs
⅓ cup honey
¾ cup walnuts, coarsely chopped

Preheat the oven to 350°F. Line 8 muffin cups with paper liners.

In a large bowl, combine the almond flour, coconut flour, salt, and baking soda. In a medium bowl, whisk together the eggs and honey. Blend the wet ingredients into the almond flour mixture with a handheld mixer until thoroughly combined, then stir in the walnuts.

Scoop ¼ cup of batter into each prepared muffin cup.

Bake for 18 to 22 minutes, until a toothpick inserted into the center of a cupcake comes out with just a few moist crumbs attached. Let the cupcakes cool in the pan for 1 hour, then frost and serve.

Almond Poppy Seed Cupcakes

MAKES 10 ❧ SWEETNESS: MEDIUM

The idea for this unique flavor combination came from our friends over at Kim and Jake's Cakes, a fabulous bakery here in Boulder, Colorado. For a finishing touch, top with Cream Cheese Frosting (page 95), or leave them plain and serve alongside eggs and fruit salad for a delightfully wholesome, yet elegant brunch.

1 cup blanched almond flour
2 tablespoons coconut flour
1/4 teaspoon sea salt
1/2 teaspoon baking soda
4 large eggs
1/2 cup agave nectar
1 teaspoon almond extract
1 tablespoon poppy seeds

Preheat the oven to 350°F. Line 10 muffin cups with paper liners.

In a large bowl, combine the almond flour, coconut flour, salt, and baking soda. In a medium bowl, whisk together the eggs, agave nectar, and almond extract. Blend the wet ingredients into the almond flour mixture with a handheld mixer until thoroughly combined, then fold in the poppy seeds.

Scoop 1/4 cup of batter into each prepared muffin cup.

Bake for 15 to 18 minutes, until a toothpick inserted into the center of a cupcake comes out with just a few moist crumbs attached. Let the cupcakes cool in the pan for 1 hour, then frost and serve.

Banana Pecan Cupcakes

MAKES 9 ❧ SWEETNESS: LOW

Light and nutty, these purely fruit-sweetened cupcakes are perfect with brunch, and quite the showstopper smothered with Whipped Cream Frosting (page 93) or Banana Whipped Cream Frosting (page 93).

$^1/_4$ cup coconut flour

2 tablespoons arrowroot powder

$^1/_4$ teaspoon sea salt

$^1/_2$ teaspoon baking soda

3 large eggs

$^1/_4$ cup coconut oil, melted over very low heat

1 cup (2 to 3) mashed very ripe bananas

3 dates, pitted

10 drops stevia

$^1/_2$ cup pecans, toasted and chopped

Preheat the oven to 350°F. Line 9 muffin cups with paper liners.

In a large bowl, combine the coconut flour, arrowroot powder, salt, and baking soda. In a high-powered blender, combine the eggs, coconut oil, bananas, dates, and stevia, then blend on the highest speed until smooth. Scrape the banana mixture into the bowl with the dry ingredients and mix together with a large spoon, until well combined, then stir in the pecans.

Scoop $^1/_4$ cup of batter into each prepared muffin cup.

Bake for 20 to 25 minutes, until a toothpick inserted into the center of a cupcake comes out with just a few moist crumbs attached. Let the cupcakes cool in the pan for 1 hour, then frost and serve.

SPECIAL OCCASION CUPCAKES

German Chocolate Cupcakes

MAKES 9 ❧ SWEETNESS: HIGH

German chocolate cake did not originate in Germany—according to
The Dictionary of American Food and Drink, it was invented by a reader
of a Dallas newspaper in 1957. This treat is typically laden with sugar
and evaporated milk. Enjoy my gluten-free, dairy-free version instead.

BATTER

1/4 cup coconut flour

1/4 cup unsweetened cocoa powder

1/4 teaspoon sea salt

1/2 teaspoon baking soda

4 large eggs

1/4 cup grapeseed oil

1/2 cup agave nectar

Coconut Pecan Filling (page 98)

Chocolate Ganache (page 92)

2 tablespoons unsweetened shredded coconut

Preheat the oven to 350°F. Line 9 muffin cups with paper liners.

To make the batter, in a large bowl, combine the coconut flour, cocoa powder, salt, and baking soda. In a medium bowl, whisk together the eggs, grapeseed oil, and agave nectar. Blend the wet ingredients into the coconut flour mixture with a hand-held mixer until thoroughly combined.

Scoop 1/4 cup of batter into each prepared muffin cup.

Bake for 18 to 22 minutes, until a toothpick inserted into the center of a cupcake comes out with just a few moist crumbs attached. Let the cupcakes cool in the pan for 1 hour.

To assemble the cupcakes, remove each from its liner. Use a serrated knife to split each cupcake in half horizontally. Spoon 1 tablespoon of Coconut Pecan Filling onto the bottom half of each cupcake. Replace the tops, pressing down to distribute the filling. Spread the sides of each cupcake with Chocolate Ganache, then spread the top of each cupcake with the remaining Coconut Pecan Filling. Sprinkle each cupcake with shredded coconut. Serve immediately.

Black Forest Cupcakes

MAKES 9 ❧ SWEETNESS: HIGH

Chocolate cake with a whipped cream center is then topped with chocolate frosting, more whipped cream, chocolate shavings, and a cherry.

BATTER

¹/₄ cup coconut flour

¹/₄ cup unsweetened cocoa powder

¹/₄ teaspoon sea salt

¹/₂ teaspoon baking soda

4 large eggs

¹/₄ cup grapeseed oil

¹/₂ cup agave nectar

1 (3-ounce) dark chocolate bar (73% cacao)

Whipped Cream Frosting (page 93)

Vegan Chocolate Frosting (page 92)

9 cherries, fresh or frozen

❧

Preheat the oven to 350°F. Line 9 muffin cups with paper liners.

To make the batter, in a large bowl, combine the coconut flour, cocoa powder, salt, and baking soda. In a medium bowl, whisk together the eggs, grapeseed oil, and agave nectar. Blend the wet ingredients into the coconut flour mixture with a hand-held mixer until thoroughly combined.

Scoop ¹/₄ cup of batter into each prepared muffin cup.

Bake for 18 to 22 minutes, until a toothpick inserted into the center of a cupcake comes out with just a few moist crumbs attached. Let the cupcakes cool in the pan for 1 hour.

To make chocolate shavings, break off a 2 by 3-inch portion of the chocolate bar. Use a vegetable peeler to carve shavings by running the blade along the long side of the chocolate piece to create a thin spiral. Repeat until you have 2 to 3 tablespoons of shavings.

To assemble the cupcakes, remove each from its liner. Use a serrated knife to split the cupcakes in half horizontally. Spoon 1 heaping tablespoon of the Whipped Cream Frosting onto the bottom half of each cupcake. Spread the top of each cupcake with the Vegan Chocolate Frosting and replace the tops. Add a large dollop (equivalent to 2 tablespoons) of Whipped Cream Frosting on top of the Vegan Chocolate Frosting. Sprinkle with chocolate shavings, finish with a cherry, and serve immediately.

Baseball Cupcakes

MAKES 9 ❧ SWEETNESS: MEDIUM

I love decorating desserts and making snacks for my son's baseball team each season, so these healthy yet festive chocolate cupcakes are near and dear to my heart. Change your frosting color, and you can create desserts for tennis, basketball, or soccer celebrations. The list goes on. . . .

BATTER

1/4 cup coconut flour
1/4 cup unsweetened cocoa powder
1/4 teaspoon sea salt
1/2 teaspoon baking soda
4 large eggs
1/4 cup grapeseed oil
1/2 cup agave nectar

Cream Cheese Frosting (page 95)
11/2 teaspoons red food coloring, made from vegetable dye

Preheat the oven to 350°F. Line 9 muffin cups with paper liners.

To make the batter, in a large bowl, combine the coconut flour, cocoa powder, salt, and baking soda. In a medium bowl, whisk together the eggs, grapeseed oil, and agave nectar. Blend the wet ingredients into the coconut flour mixture with a handheld mixer until thoroughly combined.

Scoop 1/4 cup of batter into each prepared muffin cup.

Bake for 18 to 22 minutes, until a toothpick inserted into the center of a cupcake comes out with just a few moist crumbs attached. Let the cupcakes cool in the pan for 1 hour.

To decorate, reserve 1/2 cup of Cream Cheese Frosting to use for the baseball stitches. Frost the tops of the cupcakes with the remaining Cream Cheese Frosting. Place the reserved 1/2 cup of frosting in a bowl and mix with the red food coloring, until the frosting becomes red. Spoon the red frosting into a pastry bag fitted with a plain tip and pipe a little curved red stripe onto each side of the top of each cupcake. Next, pipe the "stitches" of the baseball over the stripes. Serve immediately.

Cream-Filled Chocolate Cupcakes

MAKES 9 ❋ SWEETNESS: HIGH

Do you remember eating Hostess's prepackaged cupcakes with a cream-filled center? My version comes without the chemicals and preservatives.

BATTER

¹/₄ cup coconut flour
¹/₄ cup unsweetened cocoa powder
¹/₄ teaspoon sea salt
¹/₂ teaspoon baking soda
4 large eggs
¹/₄ cup grapeseed oil
¹/₂ cup agave nectar

Meringue Frosting (page 96)
Chocolate Ganache (page 92)

❋

Preheat the oven to 350°F. Line 9 muffin cups with paper liners.

To make the batter, in a large bowl, combine the coconut flour, cocoa powder, salt, and baking soda. In a medium bowl, whisk together the eggs, grapeseed oil, and agave nectar. Blend the wet ingredients into the coconut flour mixture with a hand-held mixer until thoroughly combined.

Scoop ¹/₄ cup of batter into each prepared muffin cup.

Bake for 18 to 22 minutes, until a toothpick inserted into the center of a cupcake comes out with just a few moist crumbs attached. Let the cupcakes cool in the pan for 1 hour.

To assemble the cupcakes, remove each from its liner. Flip each cupcake upside down, and use a paring knife to carve out a circle just a bit larger than the size of a quarter and about 1 inch deep in the bottom center of each cupcake. Save the bottom pieces to reseal the cupcakes after filling. Use the knife to hollow out a bit more around the inside of the cupcakes, discarding the crumbs.

Fill a pastry bag with the Meringue Frosting. Insert the tip of the pastry bag into the cupcake cavities and squeeze to fill. Trim the cupcake bottom pieces to make them thinner, then seal the cupcakes with the bottom pieces.

Frost the cupcake tops with the Chocolate Ganache to a smooth finish, then decorate with the remaining Meringue Frosting, making a curlicue pattern across the top of each cupcake. Serve immediately.

Banana Split Cupcakes

MAKES 8 ◌ SWEETNESS: HIGH

A sundae in a cupcake? Yes, please! Light and fluffy strawberry cup-cakes make this twist on a classic dessert a fun addition to any party. Assemble beforehand or set out bowls of all the toppings and let your guests customize their own cupcakes.

BATTER
$1/2$ cup coconut flour
1 tablespoon arrowroot powder
$1/4$ teaspoon sea salt
$1/2$ teaspoon baking soda
4 large eggs
$1/2$ cup agave nectar
1 tablespoon vanilla extract
$1/2$ cup finely chopped fresh strawberries

Chocolate Ganache (page 92)
Whipped Cream Frosting (page 93)
Gluten-free chocolate sprinkles
1 banana, cut into 16 slices
8 cherries (fresh or frozen)

Preheat the oven to 350°F. Line 8 muffin cups with paper liners.

To make the batter, in a large bowl, combine the coconut flour, arrowroot powder, salt, and baking soda. In a medium bowl, whisk together the eggs, agave nectar, and vanilla extract. Blend the wet ingredients into the coconut flour mixture with a handheld mixer until thoroughly combined, then fold in the strawberries.

Scoop $1/4$ cup of batter into each prepared muffin cup.

Bake for 20 to 25 minutes, until a toothpick inserted into the center of a cupcake comes out with just a few moist crumbs attached. Let the cupcakes cool in the pan for 1 hour.

To decorate the cupcakes, frost the tops with a layer of Chocolate Ganache. Pipe or add a big dollop of Whipped Cream Frosting (equivalent to 2 heaping tablespoons) on top of each cupcake, then cover with chocolate sprinkles. Place 2 banana slices in the whipped cream on each cupcake. Top with a cherry and serve immediately.

Ice Cream Cone Cupcakes

MAKES 10 ❧ SWEETNESS: HIGH

Baked inside gluten-free ice cream cones (see Sources, page 100), these cupcakes are a fun-filled novelty. Get creative with your own favorite frostings and don't forget the sprinkles!

10 gluten-free flat-bottomed wafer cones

BATTER
$1/2$ cup coconut flour
$1/2$ teaspoon sea salt
$1/4$ teaspoon baking soda
4 large eggs
$1/2$ cup grapeseed oil
$1/2$ cup agave nectar
1 tablespoon vanilla extract

Vegan Chocolate Frosting (page 92)
Gluten-free sprinkles

Preheat the oven to 350°F with a rack on the lowest position in the oven.

To secure the ice cream cones, tear ten 6 by 12-inch pieces of foil, one for each cone. Place a cone in the muffin cup, crumple the square of foil, and gently press around the base so the cone is securely standing upright. This will help keep the cone stable and prevent the batter from spilling out during baking. Repeat with all the cones.

To make the batter, in a large bowl, combine the coconut flour, salt, and baking soda. In a medium bowl, whisk together the eggs, grapeseed oil, agave nectar, and vanilla extract. Blend the wet ingredients into the coconut flour mixture with a hand-held mixer until thoroughly combined.

Fill each cone with a scant $1/4$ cup of batter.

Bake for 23 to 27 minutes, on the lowest rack of the oven, until a toothpick inserted into the center of a cupcake comes out with just a few moist crumbs attached.

Remove the cupcakes from the muffin pan immediately. Cool for 1 hour, then frost with Vegan Chocolate Frosting (or other frosting), top with sprinkles, and serve right away.

Independence Day Cupcakes

MAKES 9 ❧ SWEETNESS: MEDIUM

Celebrate the Fourth of July in healthy style with this very berry-bedecked vanilla cupcake. Berries will be in their prime for this gorgeous, patriotic dessert.

BATTER

1/2 cup plus 2 tablespoons coconut flour
1/2 teaspoon sea salt
1/4 teaspoon baking soda
4 large eggs
1/3 cup grapeseed oil
1/2 cup agave nectar
1 tablespoon vanilla extract

Whipped Cream Frosting (page 93)
1/2 cup fresh blueberries
1/2 cup hulled and halved fresh strawberries

Preheat the oven to 350°F. Line 9 muffin cups with paper liners.

To make the batter, in a large bowl, combine the coconut flour, salt, and baking soda. In a medium bowl, whisk together the eggs, grapeseed oil, agave nectar, and vanilla extract. Blend the wet ingredients into the coconut flour mixture with a hand-held mixer until thoroughly combined.

Scoop 1/4 cup of batter into each pre-pared muffin cup.

Bake for 18 to 22 minutes, until a tooth-pick inserted into the center of a cupcake comes out with just a few moist crumbs attached. Let the cupcakes cool in the pan for 1 hour.

To decorate, top each cupcake with a big dollop of Whipped Cream Frosting or pipe the frosting onto the cupcakes. Distribute the blueberries and strawberries over the frosted cupcakes and serve immediately.

Halloween Cupcakes

MAKES 9 ❁ SWEETNESS: MEDIUM

Much more wholesome than the usual Halloween candy, these cupcakes will captivate your little ghosts and goblins.

BATTER

1/4 cup coconut flour
1/4 cup unsweetened cocoa powder
1/4 teaspoon sea salt
1/2 teaspoon baking soda
4 large eggs
1/4 cup grapeseed oil
1/2 cup agave nectar

Orange Cream Cheese Frosting (page 96)
Gluten-free chocolate sprinkles

Preheat the oven to 350°F. Line 9 muffin cups with paper liners.

To make the batter, in a large bowl, combine the coconut flour, cocoa powder, salt, and baking soda. In a medium bowl, whisk together the eggs, grapeseed oil, and agave nectar. Blend the wet ingredients into the coconut flour mixture with a hand-held mixer until thoroughly combined.

Scoop 1/4 cup of batter into each prepared muffin cup.

Bake for 18 to 22 minutes, until a toothpick inserted into the center of a cupcake comes out with just a few moist crumbs attached. Let the cupcakes cool in the pan for 1 hour.

To decorate, frost with Orange Cream Cheese Frosting, top with chocolate sprinkles, and serve immediately.

Valentine's Cupcakes

MAKES 9 ✃ SWEETNESS: MEDIUM

Dreamy whipped cream coupled with luscious chocolate ganache makes these cupcakes enticing for your Valentine.

BATTER

¹/₄ cup coconut flour

¹/₄ cup unsweetened cocoa powder

¹/₄ teaspoon sea salt

¹/₂ teaspoon baking soda

4 large eggs

¹/₄ cup grapeseed oil

¹/₂ cup agave nectar

6 tablespoons raspberry fruit spread

Chocolate Ganache (page 92)

Whipped Cream Frosting (page 93)

1 cup fresh raspberries

¹/₄ cup mini chocolate chips (semisweet)

Preheat the oven to 350°F. Line 9 muffin cups with paper liners.

To make the batter, in a large bowl, combine the coconut flour, cocoa powder, salt, and baking soda. In a medium bowl, whisk together the eggs, grapeseed oil, and agave nectar. Blend the wet ingredients into the coconut flour mixture with a hand-held mixer until thoroughly combined.

Scoop ¹/₄ cup of batter into each prepared muffin cup.

Bake for 18 to 22 minutes, until a toothpick inserted into the center of a cupcake comes out with just a few moist crumbs attached. Let the cupcakes cool in the pan for 1 hour.

To assemble the cupcakes, remove each from its liner. Flip each cupcake upside down, and use a paring knife to carve out a circle just a bit larger than the size of a quarter and about 1 inch deep in the bottom center of each cupcake. Save the bottom pieces to reseal the cupcakes after filling. Use the knife to hollow out a bit more around the inside of the cupcakes, discarding the crumbs.

Place 2 teaspoons of fruit spread into the cavity of each cupcake. Trim the cupcake bottom pieces to make them thinner, then seal the cupcakes with the bottom pieces.

Frost the cupcake tops with the Chocolate Ganache. Top with the Whipped Cream Frosting, cover with raspberries, sprinkle with mini chocolate chips, and serve immediately.

SAVORY TREATS

Scallion Goat Cheese Muffins

MAKES 10

These versatile treats make fabulous hors d'oeuvres or a great break-fast on the run. They are so portable that they pack equally well for picnics, the office, and school lunches.

1½ cups blanched almond flour

1 teaspoon sea salt

½ teaspoon baking soda

½ teaspoon black pepper

¼ cup olive oil

3 large eggs

½ cup thinly sliced scallions, white and green parts

5 ounces goat cheese (10 tablespoons)

Preheat the oven to 350°F. Line 10 muffin cups with paper liners.

In a large bowl, combine the almond flour, salt, baking soda, and black pepper. In a medium bowl, whisk together the olive oil and eggs. Blend the wet ingredients into the almond flour mixture with a handheld mixer until thoroughly combined, then stir in the scallions.

Scoop 3 tablespoons of batter into each prepared muffin cup, then press 1 table-spoon of goat cheese into each muffin.

Bake for 20 to 25 minutes, until a tooth-pick inserted ½ inch from the edge of the muffin (to avoid the goat cheese center) comes out with just a few moist crumbs attached. Let the muffins cool in the pan for 20 minutes, then serve.

Scallion Goat Cheese Muffins and Garlic Cheddar Muffins (page 86)

Garlic Cheddar Muffins

MAKES 9

Piquant garlic and creamy cheddar make this muffin a mouthwatering appetizer or an excellent accompaniment to soup or salad. *Pictured on page 85.*

1¼ cups blanched almond flour

¼ teaspoon sea salt

½ teaspoon baking soda

2 large eggs

2 tablespoons olive oil

2 cups firmly packed grated cheddar cheese (8 ounces)

3 medium cloves garlic, pressed

Preheat the oven to 350°F. Line 9 muffin cups with paper liners.

In a large bowl, combine the almond flour, salt, and baking soda. In a medium bowl, whisk together the eggs and olive oil. Stir the wet ingredients into the almond flour mixture with a large spoon until thoroughly combined, then stir in the cheese and garlic.

Scoop ¼ cup of batter into each prepared muffin cup.

Bake for 18 to 23 minutes, until a toothpick inserted into the center of a muffin comes out with just a few moist crumbs attached. Let the muffins cool in the pan for 15 minutes, then serve.

Spinach Feta Muffins

MAKES 12

From the beloved Greek pairing of spinach and feta comes this tantalizing combination of flavors. For a fast, elegant appetizer, whip up a batch of these as mini muffins—skip the paper liners, copiously grease the pan with oil, scoop 1 tablespoon of batter into each cup, and bake at 400°F for 6 to 8 minutes, then let them cool while you are mixing drinks. The yield is approximately 40 mini muffins.

1 1/2 cups blanched almond flour
1 tablespoon arrowroot powder
1 teaspoon sea salt
1/2 teaspoon baking soda
1/4 cup olive oil
3 large eggs
1 cup fresh spinach, chopped
8 ounces feta cheese, crumbled

Preheat the oven to 350°F. Line 12 muffin cups with paper liners.

In a large bowl, combine the almond flour, arrowroot powder, salt, and baking soda. In a medium bowl, whisk together the olive oil and eggs. Blend the wet ingredients into the almond flour mixture with a handheld mixer until thoroughly combined, then stir in the spinach and fold in the feta.

Scoop 1/4 cup of batter into each prepared muffin cup.

Bake for 22 to 27 minutes, until a toothpick inserted into the center of a muffin comes out with just a few moist crumbs attached. Let the muffins cool in the pan for 20 minutes, then serve.

Parmesan Muffins

MAKES 11

These addictive Parmesan muffins are excellent with eggs for brunch or served as a dinner roll.

1¹/₂ cups blanched almond flour

1 teaspoon sea salt

¹/₂ teaspoon baking soda

1 tablespoon Spice Hunter Italian Seasoning

¹/₄ cup olive oil

3 large eggs

2¹/₄ cups grated Parmesan cheese (8 ounces)

Preheat the oven to 350°F. Line 11 muffin cups with paper liners.

In a large bowl, combine the almond flour, salt, baking soda, and Italian seasoning. In a medium bowl, whisk together the olive oil and eggs. Blend the wet ingredients into the almond flour mixture with a handheld mixer until thoroughly combined, then stir in the Parmesan.

Scoop ¹/₄ cup of batter into each prepared muffin cup.

Bake for 20 to 25 minutes, until a toothpick inserted into the center of a muffin comes out with just a few moist crumbs attached. Let the muffins cool in the pan for 20 minutes, then serve.

Chive Pepper Muffins

MAKES 8

Spicy chive- and pepper-flecked savory muffins are a wonderful dairy-free option to pair with soup or salad. Sliced in half and loaded with your favorite leftovers, they make a delectable sandwich.

1½ cups blanched almond flour
1 teaspoon sea salt
½ teaspoon baking soda
1 tablespoon black pepper
¼ cup olive oil
3 large eggs
½ cup finely chopped fresh chives

Preheat the oven to 350°F. Line 8 muffin cups with paper liners.

In a large bowl, combine the almond flour, salt, baking soda, and black pepper. In a medium bowl, whisk together the olive oil and eggs. Blend the wet ingredients into the almond flour mixture with a handheld mixer until thoroughly combined, then stir in the chives.

Scoop ¼ cup of batter into each prepared muffin cup.

Bake for 20 to 25 minutes, until a toothpick inserted into the center of a muffin comes out with just a few moist crumbs attached. Let the muffins cool in the pan for 20 minutes, then serve.

Breakfast Bran Muffins

MAKES 11 ❖ SWEETNESS: LOW

These highly nutritious breakfast muffins (made with nuts, seeds, and dried fruit) are a great alternative to store-bought breakfast bars and granola bars because they're fresh, free of packaging, and cost-effective. Enjoy them while they're still warm!

1/2 cup blanched almond flour

1/2 cup flax meal

1/4 teaspoon sea salt

1/2 teaspoon baking soda

6 dates, pitted

3 large eggs

2 tablespoons olive oil

1/4 cup water

1/4 cup pumpkin seeds

1/4 cup sesame seeds

1/4 cup sunflower seeds

1/2 cup walnuts, chopped

1/2 cup currants

Preheat the oven to 350°F. Line 11 muffin cups with paper liners.

In a large bowl, combine the almond flour, flax meal, salt, and baking soda. In a high-powered blender, puree the dates, eggs, olive oil, and water on high speed until very smooth. Stir the wet ingredients into the almond flour mixture until blended, then stir in the seeds, walnuts, and currants.

Scoop 1/4 cup of batter into each prepared muffin cup.

Bake for 15 to 20 minutes, until a toothpick inserted into the center of a muffin comes out with just a few moist crumbs attached. Let the muffins cool in the pan for 20 minutes, then serve warm.

FROSTINGS, FILLINGS, AND TOPPINGS

Vegan Chocolate Frosting

MAKES 1¼ CUPS ❧ SWEETNESS: HIGH

Who would guess that this super-rich and thick chocolate frosting is vegan? Frost over everything, or simply eat it with a spoon, like I do.

6 ounces dark chocolate chips (73% cacao) (about 1 heaping cup)

½ cup Spectrum all-vegetable shortening

¼ cup agave nectar

1 tablespoon vanilla extract

2 tablespoons water

Pinch of sea salt

In a medium saucepan over very low heat, melt the chocolate until smooth. Allow the pan to stand on the counter for 5 to 10 minutes to cool the chocolate to room temperature.

Blend in the shortening with a handheld mixer, then blend in the agave nectar, vanilla extract, water, and salt until smooth. Place the saucepan in the refrigerator for 3 to 8 minutes, until the frosting becomes spreadable.

If the frosting becomes too stiff to work with, reheat the pan ever so briefly over very low heat and stir until the frosting is softened. If the frosting is too runny, place it back in the refrigerator until it firms up.

Use immediately or store in a glass Mason jar in the refrigerator for up to 3 days.

Chocolate Ganache

MAKES ¾ CUP ❧ SWEETNESS: MEDIUM

According to *Joy of Cooking*, a ganache is a sleek, rich coating on a European torte, or the center of a rich chocolate truffle. I have adapted the old standard from this amazing cookbook, which is the most dog-eared in my collection. I like this recipe best with Triple Chocolate Cupcakes (page 33) or Almond Fudge Cupcakes (page 38).

¾ cup heavy cream

8 ounces dark chocolate chips (73% cacao) (just over 1⅓ cups)

1 teaspoon vanilla extract

Pinch of sea salt

In a medium saucepan, bring the heavy cream to a boil, then immediately remove it from the heat. Stir in the chocolate until it is melted and smooth, then stir in the vanilla extract and salt.

Let the ganache stand at room temperature for 5 minutes, then transfer to the refrigerator and chill until the ganache thickens and becomes shiny and spreadable. This could take anywhere from 10 to 30 minutes, depending on the temperature of your refrigerator.

If the frosting becomes too stiff to work with, reheat the pan ever so briefly over very low heat, and stir until softened.

Use immediately or store in a glass Mason jar in the refrigerator for up to 24 hours.

Whipped Cream Frosting

MAKES 2 CUPS ⊰⊱ SWEETNESS: MEDIUM

An ultra-versatile classic, use whipped cream frosting on Strawberry Cupcakes (page 24) to create little strawberry shortcakes, on Apple Spice Cupcakes (page 60) for a taste of mini apple pie, or on just about any other cupcake to turn an everyday delight into elegant perfection.

1 cup heavy cream
2 tablespoons agave nectar

In a deep bowl, whip the cream and agave nectar with a handheld mixer for 2 to 3 minutes, until it is thick and fluffy and soft peaks form.

    Use immediately, using a spoon for dollops or a pastry bag for swirls. Or store in a glass Mason jar in the refrigerator for up to 24 hours.

Banana Whipped Cream Frosting

MAKES 3 CUPS ⊰⊱ SWEETNESS: HIGH

My older son created this recipe, which is incredible over Chocolate Banana Cupcakes (page 37). After he made a test batch, I asked him if it needed more bananas. His reply? "There's at least one little bit of banana in every bite."

1 cup heavy cream
2 tablespoons agave nectar
1 cup (2 to 3) mashed very ripe bananas

In a deep bowl, whip the cream and agave nectar with a handheld mixer for 2 to 3 minutes, until thick, fluffy, stiff peaks form. Mix in the bananas, then whip for 20 to 30 seconds to incorporate.

    Use immediately, spooning dollops over cupcakes. Or store in a glass Mason jar in the refrigerator for up to 3 hours and use before the bananas turn brown.

Vegan Coconut Whip

MAKES 2 CUPS ⊰⊱ SWEETNESS: MEDIUM

Here's a delicious alternative to regular whipped cream made with dairy. I discovered this topping, which some refer to as "vegan whipped cream," when Sally Parrot Ashbrook left a comment on my website suggesting it. I've been hooked ever since! Be sure to use full-fat Thai Kitchen coconut milk for this recipe; the other brands I tested did not work. For an extra kick, top with unsweetened coconut flakes.

2 (13.5-ounce) cans Thai Kitchen coconut milk

$1/4$ cup agave nectar

1 tablespoon vanilla extract

Pinch of sea salt

Place the cans of coconut milk in the refrigerator overnight so they are very well chilled. Take the cans out of the refrigerator. Remove the lids from the cans entirely and gently scoop out the solid coconut cream, placing it in a bowl. Pour any remaining liquid coconut water into a jar for another use.

Whip the coconut cream with a handheld mixer for 1 minute, until light and fluffy. Whip in the agave nectar, vanilla extract, and salt.

Use immediately or store in a glass Mason jar in the refrigerator for up to 24 hours.

White Chocolate Frosting

MAKES 1 CUP ⊰⊱ SWEETNESS: HIGH

Eureka! A frosting with just two ingredients. Spread this rich, sweet, creamy frosting over Chocolate Cupcakes (page 22), Strawberry Cupcakes (page 24), or, for an extra sweet treat, White Chocolate Cherry Cupcakes (page 40).

7 ounces white chocolate chips (just less than $1^1/4$ cups)

$1/2$ cup Spectrum all-vegetable shortening

In a small saucepan over very low heat, melt the white chocolate until smooth, stirring constantly. Allow the pan to stand on the counter for 10 minutes to cool down to room temperature.

Blend in the shortening with a handheld mixer. Place the saucepan in the refrigerator for 20 minutes, until the frosting is slightly chilled and thickened.

Use immediately or store in a glass Mason jar in the refrigerator for up to 3 days. Before using, set the frosting on the counter for 1 to 2 hours, to allow it to come to room temperature, then stir with a flexible spatula until spreadable. This frosting works best at room temperature.

Vegan Buttercream

MAKES 1³/4 CUPS ⊰⊱ SWEETNESS: HIGH

Making a frosting without butter and powdered sugar is a bit of a feat; this vegan "buttercream" is worth the extra effort. If the texture is too soft, chill the frosting in the refrigerator for anywhere from 10 to 30 minutes to firm up.

1/2 cup Spectrum all-vegetable shortening

1/2 cup Earth Balance Natural Buttery Spread (soy free)

Pinch of sea salt

3/4 cup agave nectar

1 tablespoon vanilla extract

In a large bowl, blend together the shortening and buttery spread with a handheld mixer until creamy. Mix in the salt, agave nectar, and vanilla extract, whipping until smooth.

Refrigerate the frosting for 2 hours, or until firm. Remove the frosting from the refrigerator. If the frosting is too stiff to spread, place the bowl over a pan of warm water very briefly and whip the frosting until it has the desired consistency. Frost your cupcakes immediately, then place the frosted cupcakes in the refrigerator to keep the consistency of the frosting firm until serving.

You can also store the buttercream in a glass Mason jar in the refrigerator for up to 3 days. When you remove it from the refrigerator, follow the above instructions. If the frosting separates, simply whip it together with a handheld mixer until it is creamy again.

Cream Cheese Frosting

MAKES 2 CUPS ⊰⊱ SWEETNESS: LOW

Whether smothering my Red Velvet Cupcakes (page 28) or topping Zucchini Cupcakes (page 61), this simple, tangy, and rich frosting is a classic with true versatility.

3/4 cup heavy cream

8 ounces cream cheese, at room temperature

1/4 cup agave nectar

In a deep bowl, whip the cream with a handheld mixer until stiff peaks form. In a separate larger bowl, whip the cream cheese and agave nectar until well combined.

Using a rubber spatula, gently fold the whipped cream into the cream cheese mixture.

Use immediately or store in a glass Mason jar in the refrigerator for up to 2 days.

Orange Cream Cheese Frosting

MAKES 1¼ CUPS ❀ SWEETNESS: MEDIUM

This fruity orange frosting makes a deliciously decorative topping for Halloween Cupcakes (page 81) and other festive treats.

Change it up and make your own lemon cream cheese frosting by substituting lemon zest for the orange zest and eliminating the food coloring.

8 ounces cream cheese, at room temperature
½ cup butter (1 stick), at room temperature
¼ cup agave nectar
1 tablespoon firmly packed orange zest
Red food coloring, made from vegetable dye
Yellow food coloring, made from vegetable dye

In a deep bowl, whip the cream cheese, butter, and agave nectar until smooth using a handheld mixer. Add the orange zest and food coloring and mix until the desired orange hue is achieved, adding more food coloring as necessary.

Refrigerate for 30 minutes, until the frosting is slightly chilled and thickened so that it is easily spreadable.

Use immediately or store in a glass Mason jar in the refrigerator for up to 3 days.

Meringue Frosting

MAKES 3 CUPS ❀ SWEETNESS: HIGH

Making meringues is a bit of an acquired skill and it can take some practice to master the technique (see pages 12–13); however, the impressive results of this super-fluffy topping are worth every ounce of effort. Once you get it right, it's very simple to make.

¼ cup agave nectar
2 egg whites

In a small saucepan over medium heat, bring the agave nectar nectar to a boil, stirring constantly. Decrease the heat to low and simmer for 6 to 10 minutes, watching constantly and stirring occasionally, until the agave nectar darkens slightly from its original amber color, then remove from the heat and set aside.

In a deep bowl, whip the egg whites to stiff peaks using a handheld mixer. Be sure to push the beater around the bowl to incorporate air into the whites. This step is important; if your egg whites are not whipped to stiff peaks, the recipe won't work. Stop whipping as soon as the egg whites are stiff; overwhipping will result in egg whites that are dry and grainy. The foam of the whites will be stiff enough to stand up in well-defined, unwavering peaks.

Drizzle the warm agave nectar *very* slowly into the egg whites while whipping with a handheld mixer, to keep the peaks stiff. The meringue will become pearlescent and shiny. Allow to cool to room temperature, then use right away.

Strawberry Meringue Frosting

MAKES 3 CUPS ⊰⊱ SWEETNESS: HIGH

My younger son eats this straight out of the bowl!

1/4 cup agave nectar

2 egg whites

2 tablespoons finely chopped fresh strawberries

In a small saucepan over medium heat, bring the agave nectar to a boil, stirring constantly. Decrease the heat to low and simmer for 6 to 10 minutes, watching constantly and stirring occasionally, until the agave nectar darkens slightly from its original amber color, then remove from the heat and set aside.

In a deep bowl, whip the egg whites to stiff peaks using a handheld mixer. Be sure to push the beaters around the bowl to incorporate air into the whites. This step is important; if your egg whites are not whipped to stiff peaks, the recipe won't work. Stop whipping as soon as the egg whites are stiff; overwhipping will result in egg whites that are dry and grainy. The foam of the whites will be stiff enough to stand up in well-defined, unwavering peaks.

Drizzle the warm agave nectar *very* slowly into the egg whites, while whipping with a handheld mixer, to keep the peaks stiff. The meringue will become pearlescent and shiny.

Allow to cool to room temperature, then fold the strawberries into the meringue. Use right away.

Vegan Coconut Frosting

MAKES 2 CUPS ⊰⊱ SWEETNESS: MEDIUM

Pair this super-creamy, yet dairy-free frosting with Lime Cupcakes (page 55), Piña Colada Cupcakes (page 51), or Vegan Chocolate Cupcakes (page 23).

1/2 cup coconut milk

1/2 cup agave nectar

1 tablespoon arrowroot powder

1 tablespoon water

1 cup coconut oil, melted over very low heat

In a medium saucepan, bring the coconut milk and agave nectar to a boil over medium heat. Whisk the ingredients together, then decrease the heat and simmer for 2 to 3 minutes, to reduce just slightly, stirring frequently.

In a small bowl, dissolve the arrowroot powder in water, stirring to make a slurry. Increase the heat under the saucepan to medium-high so the mixture is bubbling. Add the arrowroot slurry to the coconut mixture, whisking constantly until the mixture thickens and turns opaque and shiny, about 1 minute. Once the mixture becomes shiny, remove the pan from the heat and gradually blend in the coconut oil with a handheld mixer until well combined.

Allow to cool on the counter for 15 minutes. The mixture will not look like frosting yet—don't worry; this is okay.

Chill the frosting in the refrigerator for 1 to 1 1/2 hours, until the frosting fully solidifies and looks opaque white in color. Remove from the refrigerator and whip with a handheld mixer until thick and fluffy. The frosting will be sticky looking and lumps will dissolve during whipping.

Use immediately or store in a glass Mason jar in the refrigerator for up to 3 days. Allow the frosting to soften a bit after removing from the refrigerator. Stir with a flexible spatula until spreadable.

Chocolate Dirt

MAKES 1/2 CUP ✄ SWEETNESS: LOW

Although dirt may not sound appetizing, this fun topping is perfect for dusting cakes and cupcakes. You only need one simple ingredient—dark chocolate chips. Just be sure to clean out your coffee grinder before and after making it so you don't get coffee-flavored dirt or chocolate-flavored coffee—though I could think of worse things.

1/2 cup dark chocolate chips (73% cacao)

Place the chips in a coffee grinder. Grind until they have the texture of coarse sand. Use immediately or store in a glass Mason jar at room temperature for up to 1 week.

Coconut Pecan Filling

MAKES 2 CUPS ✄ SWEETNESS: HIGH

This recipe is based on one from Martha Stewart, though mine is dairy free. Use this rich and thick coconuty filling with German Chocolate Cupcakes (page 71), or for an unexpected twist, spread over Coconut Cupcakes (page 52).

2 egg yolks
1 cup coconut milk
1/2 cup agave nectar
1/4 cup coconut oil
3/4 cup unsweetened shredded coconut
1 cup pecans, toasted and coarsely chopped

In a medium saucepan, combine the egg yolks, coconut milk, agave nectar, and coconut oil. Bring to a vigorous simmer over medium heat, stirring constantly, and cook for 5 minutes, until the mixture is slightly reduced. Strain through a sieve into a bowl.

Mix the shredded coconut and pecans into the egg yolk mixture and let cool completely, stirring every now and then.

Use immediately or store in a glass Mason jar in the refrigerator for up to 24 hours. Before using, bring to room temperature and stir with a flexible spatula until softened.

Sources

For one-stop shopping where you can buy all of the below ingredients, visit www.benefityourlife.com.

Agave Nectar

Madhava
303-823-3212
www.madhavasagave.com

Ohgave
303-588-4107
www.ohgave.com

Almond Flour

Benefit Your Life
800-295-1058
www.benefityourlife.com

Honeyville
888-810-3212
www.honeyvillegrain.com

Lucy's Kitchen Shop
888-484-2126
www.lucyskitchenshop.com

Arrowroot Powder

More Than Alive
800-516-5911
www.morethanalive.com

Buttery Spread

Earth Balance
201-421-3970
www.earthbalancenatural.com

Chocolate

365 Organic
www.wholefoodsmarket.com
Semi-sweet mini chips

Dagoba
866-972-6879
www.dagobachocolate.com
Cocoa powder/dark chocolate chips (73% cacao)

Enjoy Life
888-503-6569
www.enjoylifefoods.com
Mini chocolate chips

Sunspire
800-434-4246
www.sunspire.com
White chocolate chips

Coconut Flour

Nuts Online
800-558-6887
www.nutsonline.com

Coconut Milk

Thai Kitchen
800-967-8424
www.thaikitchen.com

Food Coloring

India Tree Natural Decorating Colors
800-369-4848
www.indiatree.com

Fruit Spread

Rigoni di Asiago FioridiFrutta
202-267-3280
http://fiordifruttausa.com/frutta.shtml

Ice Cream Cones

Let's Do Gluten Free
805-684-8500
www.edwardandsons.com

Oils and Shortening

Spectrum Naturals
800-434-4246
www.spectrumorganics.com

Salt

Selina Naturally
800-867-7258
www.celticseasalt.com
Finely ground Celtic sea salt

Sprinkles

Let's Do Gluten Free Sprinklez
805-684-8500
www.edwardandsons.com

Stevia

Sweet Leaf
800-899-9908
www.sweetleaf.com

Vanilla Extract

Flavorganics
973-344-8014
www.flavorganics.com

Yacon Syrup

Navitas Naturals
888-645-4282
www.navitasnaturals.com

Index

MEASUREMENT CONVERSION CHARTS

Volume

U.S.	Imperial	Metric
1 tablespoon	$1/2$ fl oz	15 ml
2 tablespoons	1 fl oz	30 ml
$1/4$ cup	2 fl oz	60 ml
$1/3$ cup	3 fl oz	90 ml
$1/2$ cup	4 fl oz	120 ml
$2/3$ cup	5 fl oz ($1/4$ pint)	150 ml
$3/4$ cup	6 fl oz	180 ml
1 cup	8 fl oz ($1/3$ pint)	240 ml
$1\,1/4$ cups	10 fl oz ($1/2$ pint)	300 ml
2 cups (1 pint)	16 fl oz ($2/3$ pint)	480 ml
$2\,1/2$ cups	20 fl oz (1 pint)	600 ml
1 quart	32 fl oz ($1\,2/3$ pints)	1 l

Temperature

Fahrenheit	Celsius/Gas Mark
250°F	120°C/gas mark $1/2$
275°F	135°C/gas mark 1
300°F	150°C/gas mark 2
325°F	160°C/gas mark 3
350°F	180° or 175°C/gas mark 4
375°F	190°C/gas mark 5
400°F	200°C/gas mark 6
425°F	220°C/gas mark 7
450°F	230°C/gas mark 8
475°F	245°C/gas mark 9
500°F	260°C

Length

Inch	Metric
$1/4$ inch	6 mm
$1/2$ inch	1.25 cm
$3/4$ inch	2 cm
1 inch	2.5 cm
6 inches ($1/2$ foot)	15 cm
12 inches (1 foot)	30 cm

Weight

U.S./Imperial	Metric
$1/2$ oz	15 g
1 oz	30 g
2 oz	60 g
$1/4$ lb	115 g
$1/3$ lb	150 g
$1/2$ lb	225 g
$3/4$ lb	350 g
1 lb	450 g